alanis morissette

under rug swept

© Copyright 2002 Universal Music Publishing Group

Exclusive distributors:
Music Sales Limited, 8/9 Frith Street, London W1D 3JB, England.
Music Sales Pty Limited, 120 Rothschild Avenue, Rosebery, NSW 2018, Australia.
Order No. AM974710
ISBN: 0-7119-9527-3
Unauthorised reproduction of any part of this publication by
any means including photocopying is an infringement of copyright.

Project Managers: Jeannette Delisa and Aaron Stang
Transcribed by Danny Begelman
Music Editors: Aaron Stang and Colgan Bryan
Album Design © 2002 Maverick Recording Company
Photography: Rankin
Book art layout: Martha L. Ramirez

www.musicsales.com

21 THINGS I WANT IN A LOVER

Words and Music by
ALANIS MORISSETTE

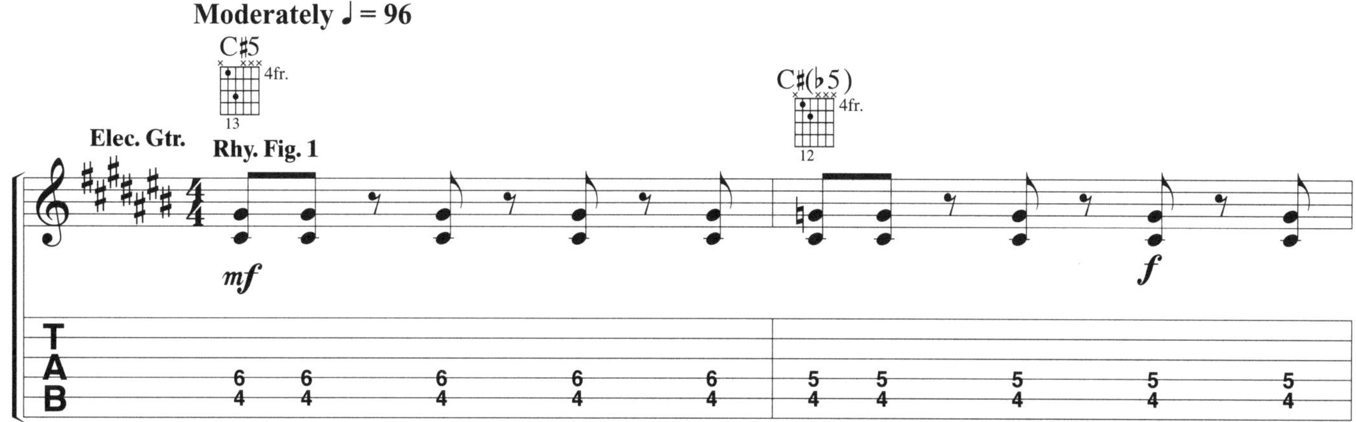

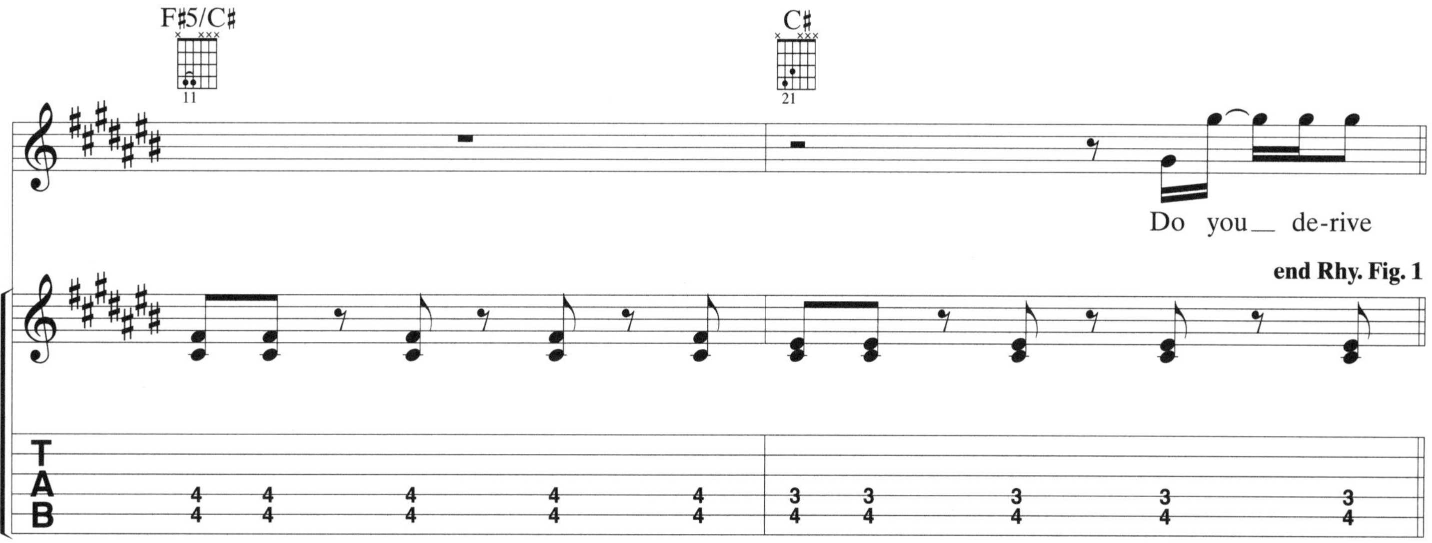

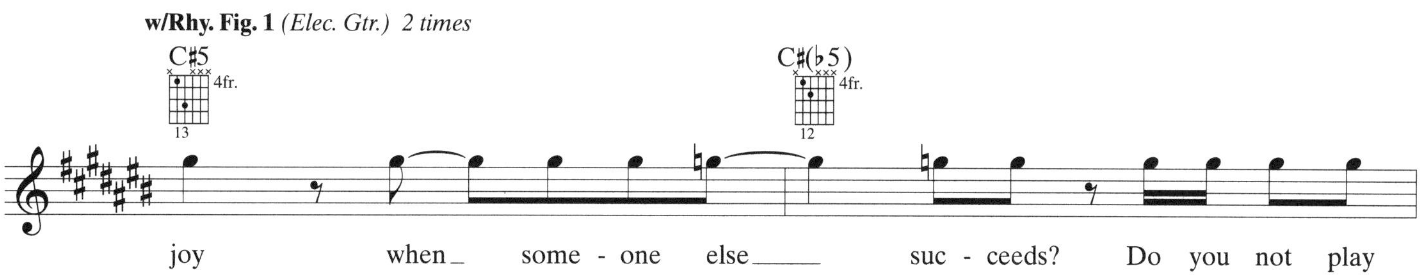

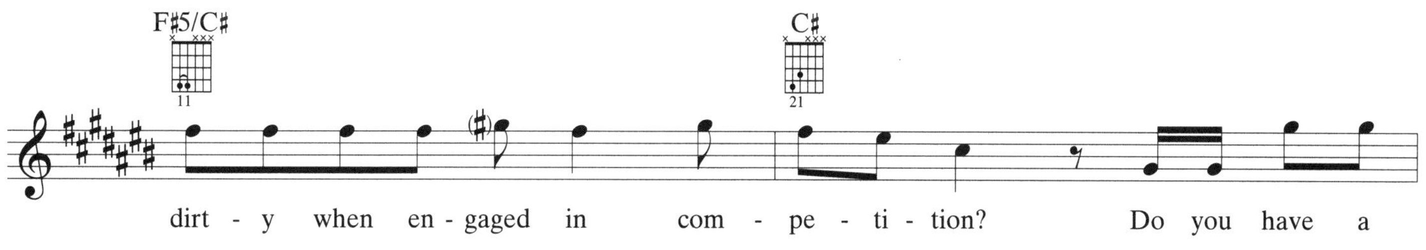

© 2002 Universal - MCA Music Publishing, A Division of Universal Studios, Inc. and 1974 Music
All Rights Controlled and Administered by Universal - MCA Music Publishing,
A Division of Universal Studios, Inc.
All Rights Reserved

C♯5
C♯(♭5)
big in - tel - lec - tu - al ca - pac - i - ty but know that
w/Rhy. Fig. 1 (Elec. Gtr.) 2 times
F♯5/C♯
C♯5
it a - lone does not e - quate wis - dom? 2. Do you see ev -
Verses 2, 3, & 4:
r'y - thing as an il - lu - sion but en - joy it
joy from div-ing in and see-ing that lov-ing
4. See additional lyrics
C♯
e - ven though you are not of it? Are you both
some-one can ac-tu-al-ly feel like free-dom? Are you fun-ny?
mas - cu-line and fem - i-nine? po - lit - i - cal - ly a - ware? and don't be -
à la self - dep - re - cat - ing? like ad - ven - ture?
lieve in cap - i - tal pun - ish - ment?
and have man-y formed o-pin-ions.?
Chorus:
Elec. Gtr.
Cont. rhy. simile
These are twen - ty one things that I want

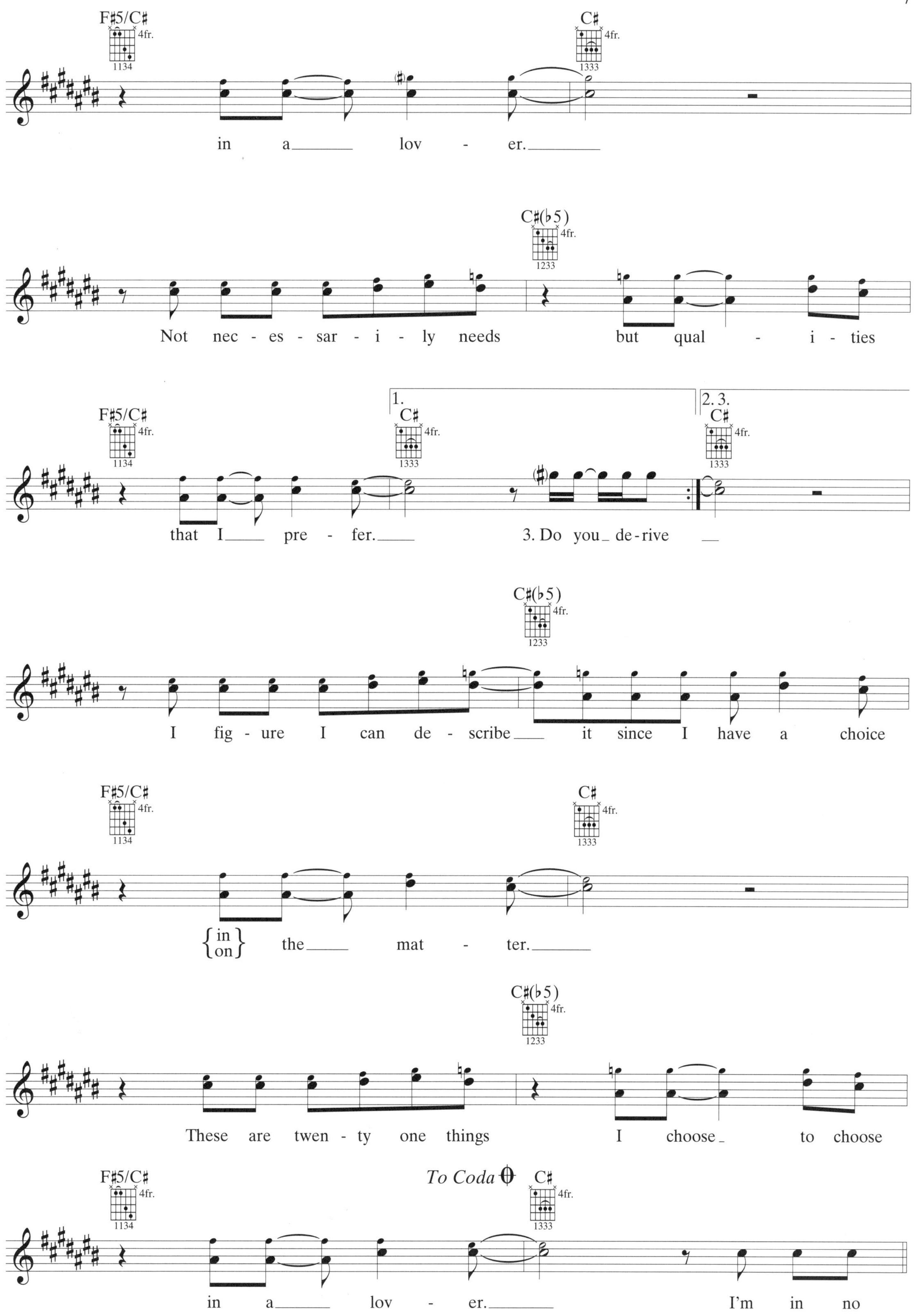
F♯5/C♯
4fr.
1134
C♯
4fr.
1333
in a lov - er.
C♯(♭5)
4fr.
1233
Not nec - es - sar - i - ly needs but qual - i - ties
F♯5/C♯
1.
C♯
2. 3.
C♯
that I pre - fer.
3. Do you de - rive
C♯(♭5)
I fig - ure I can de - scribe it since I have a choice
F♯5/C♯
C♯
in
on
the mat - ter.
C♯(♭5)
These are twen - ty one things I choose to choose
F♯5/C♯
To Coda
C♯
in a lov - er.
I'm in no

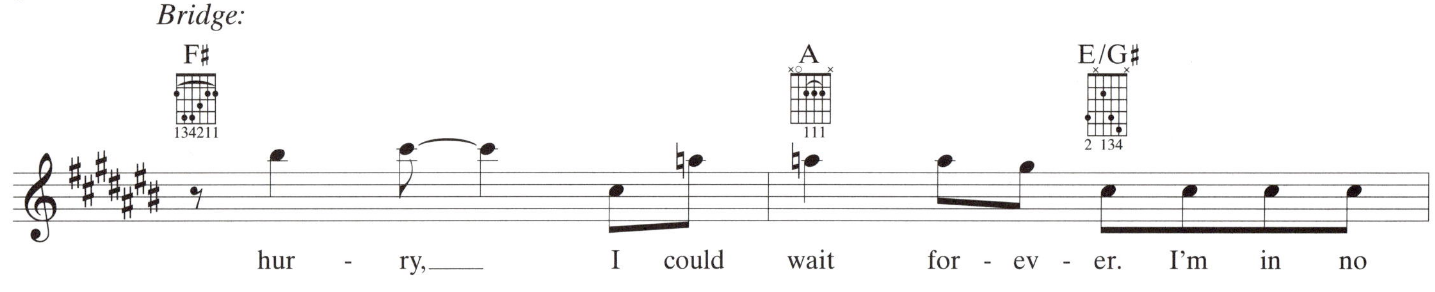

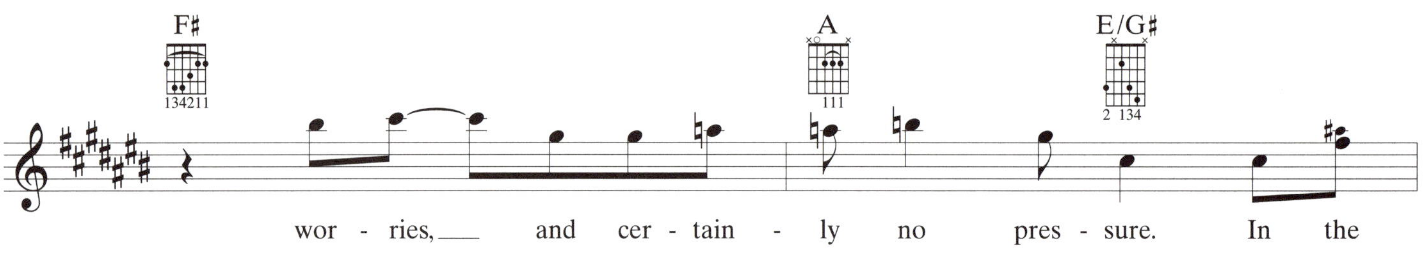

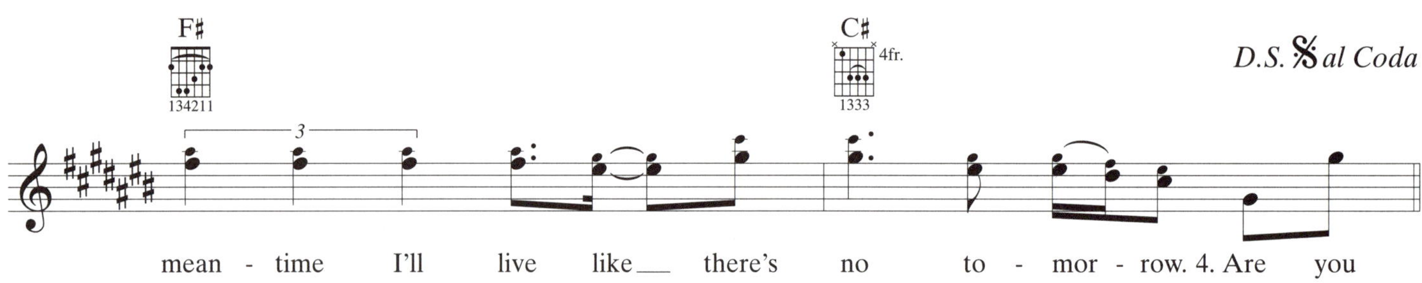

Verse 4:
Are you uninhibited in bed?
More than three times a week?
Up for being experimental?
Are you athletic?
Are you thriving in a job that helps your brother?
Are you not addicted?
(To Chorus:)

NARCISSUS

Words and Music by
ALANIS MORISSETTE

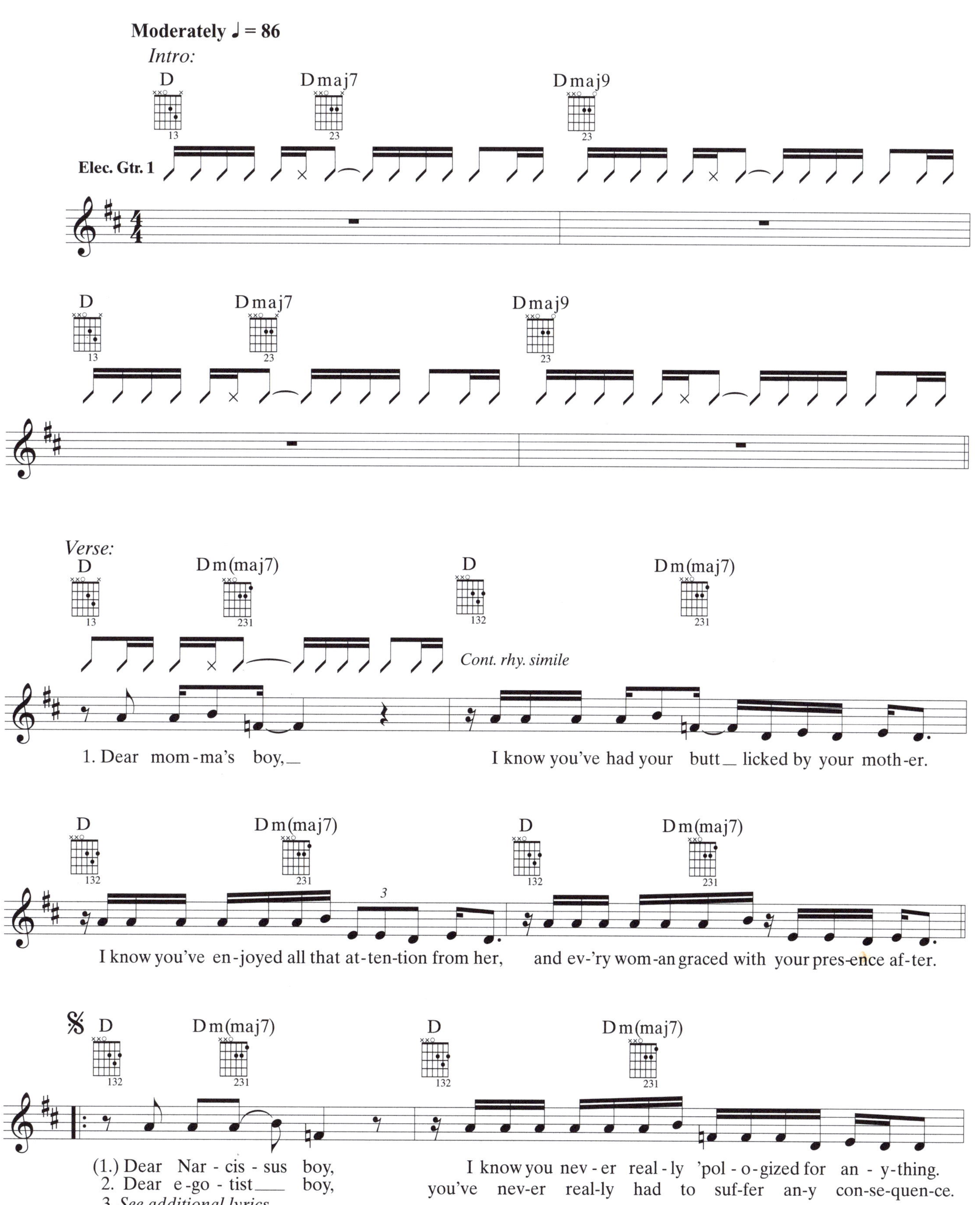

© 2002 Universal - MCA Music Publishing, A Division of Universal Studios, Inc. and 1974 Music
All Rights Controlled and Administered by Universal - MCA Music Publishing,
A Division of Universal Studios, Inc.
All Rights Reserved

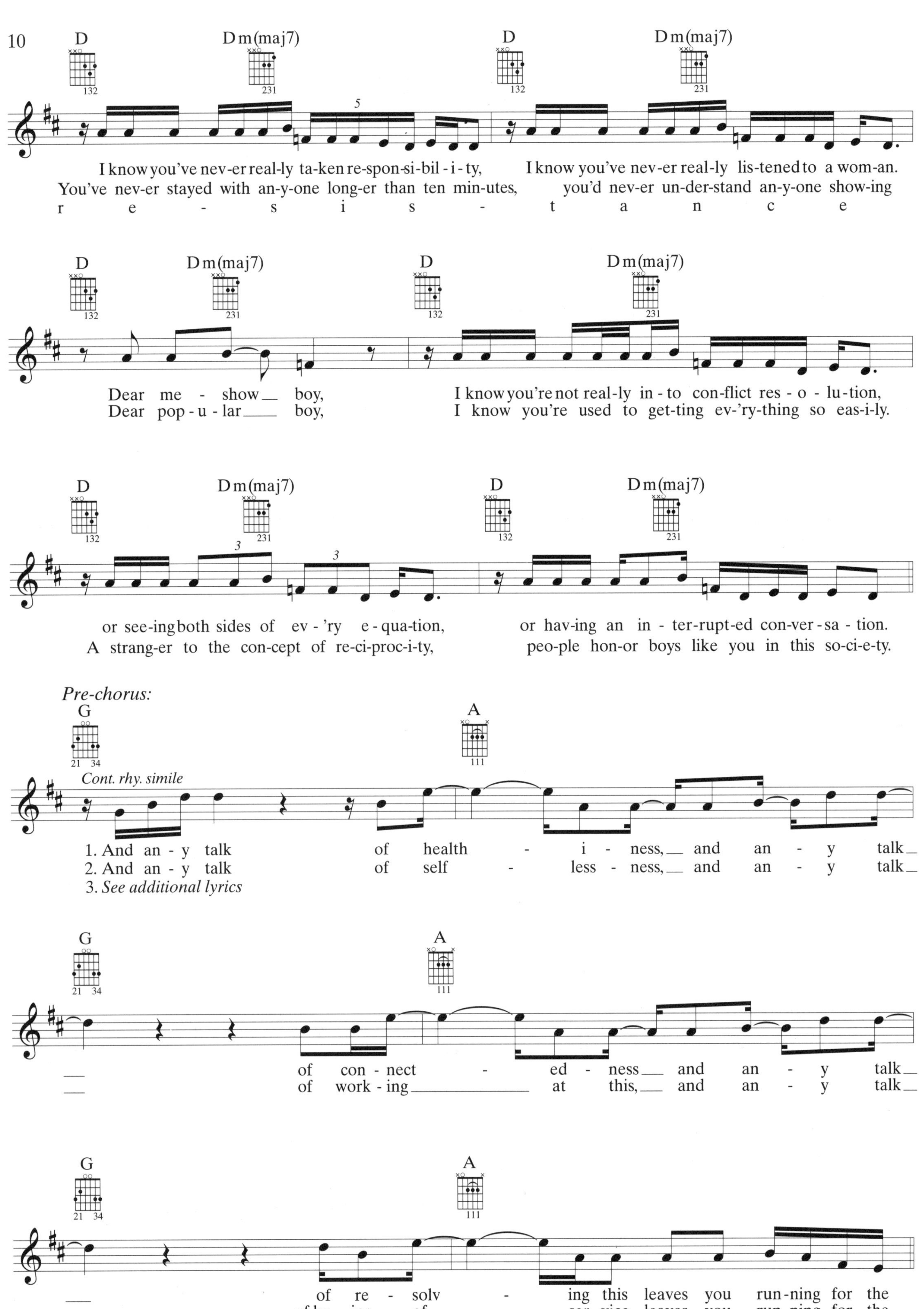
D
Dm(maj7)
I know you've nev-er real-ly ta-ken re-spon-si-bil-i-ty,
I know you've nev-er real-ly lis-tened to a wom-an.
You've nev-er stayed with an-y-one long-er than ten min-utes,
you'd nev-er un-der-stand an-y-one show-ing
r e - s i s - t a n c e
Dear me - show boy,
I know you're not real-ly in-to con-flict res-o-lu-tion,
Dear pop-u-lar boy,
I know you're used to get-ting ev-'ry-thing so eas-i-ly.
or see-ing both sides of ev-'ry e-qua-tion,
or hav-ing an in-ter-rupt-ed con-ver-sa-tion.
A strang-er to the con-cept of re-ci-proc-i-ty,
peo-ple hon-or boys like you in this so-ci-e-ty.
Pre-chorus:
G
A
Cont. rhy. simile
1. And an-y talk of health-i-ness, and an-y talk
2. And an-y talk of self-less-ness, and an-y talk
3. See additional lyrics
of con-nect-ed-ness and an-y talk
of work-ing at this, and an-y talk
of re-solv-ing this leaves you run-ning for the
of be-ing of ser-vice leaves you run-ning for the

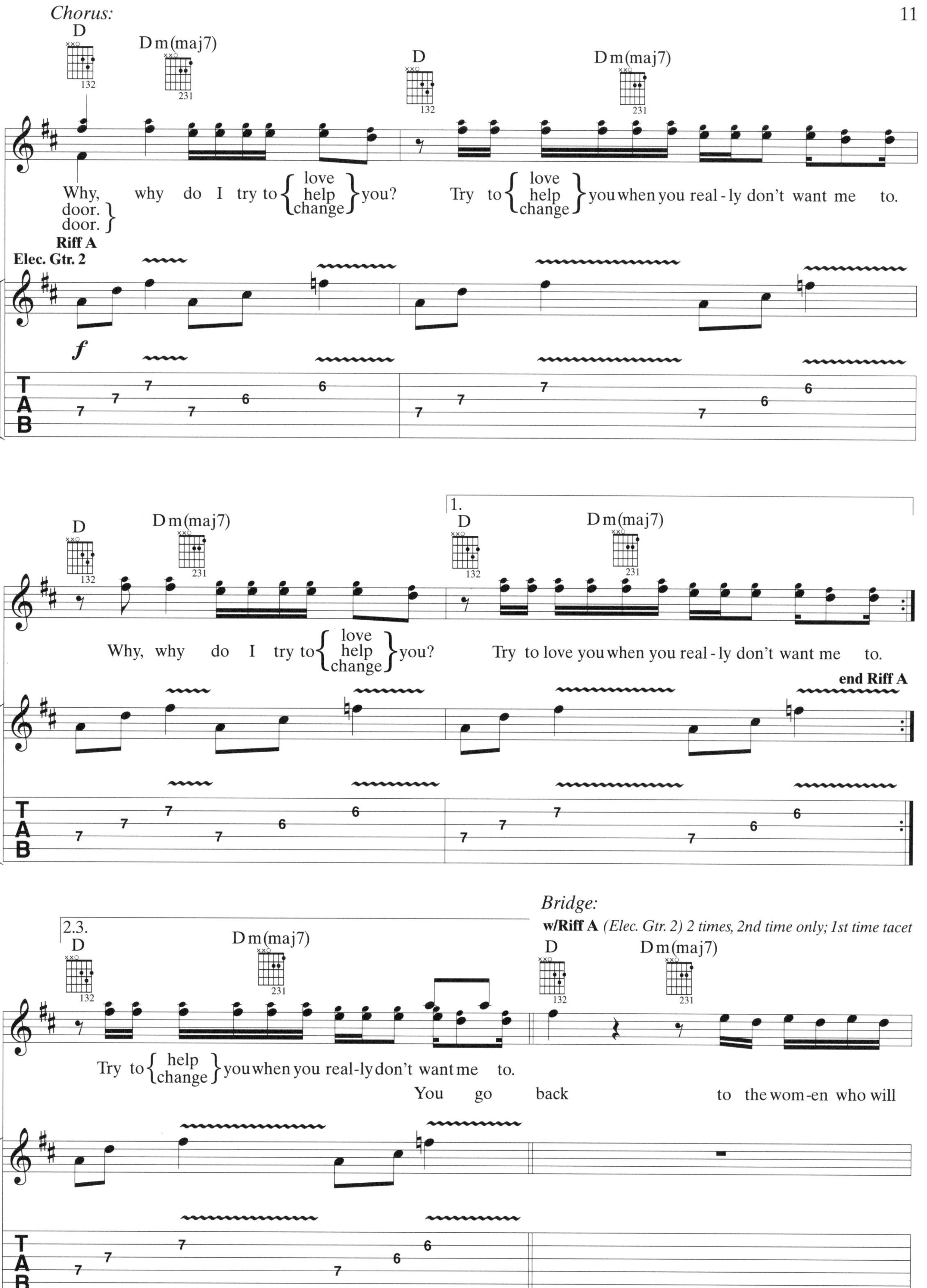

Chorus:
D
Dm(maj7)
Why, why do I try to love / help / change you? Try to love / help / change you when you real-ly don't want me to.
door.
door.
Riff A
Elec. Gtr. 2
f
1.
Why, why do I try to love / help / change you? Try to love you when you real-ly don't want me to.
end Riff A
2.3.
Try to help / change you when you real-ly don't want me to.
Bridge:
w/Riff A (Elec. Gtr. 2) 2 times, 2nd time only; 1st time tacet
You go back to the wom-en who will

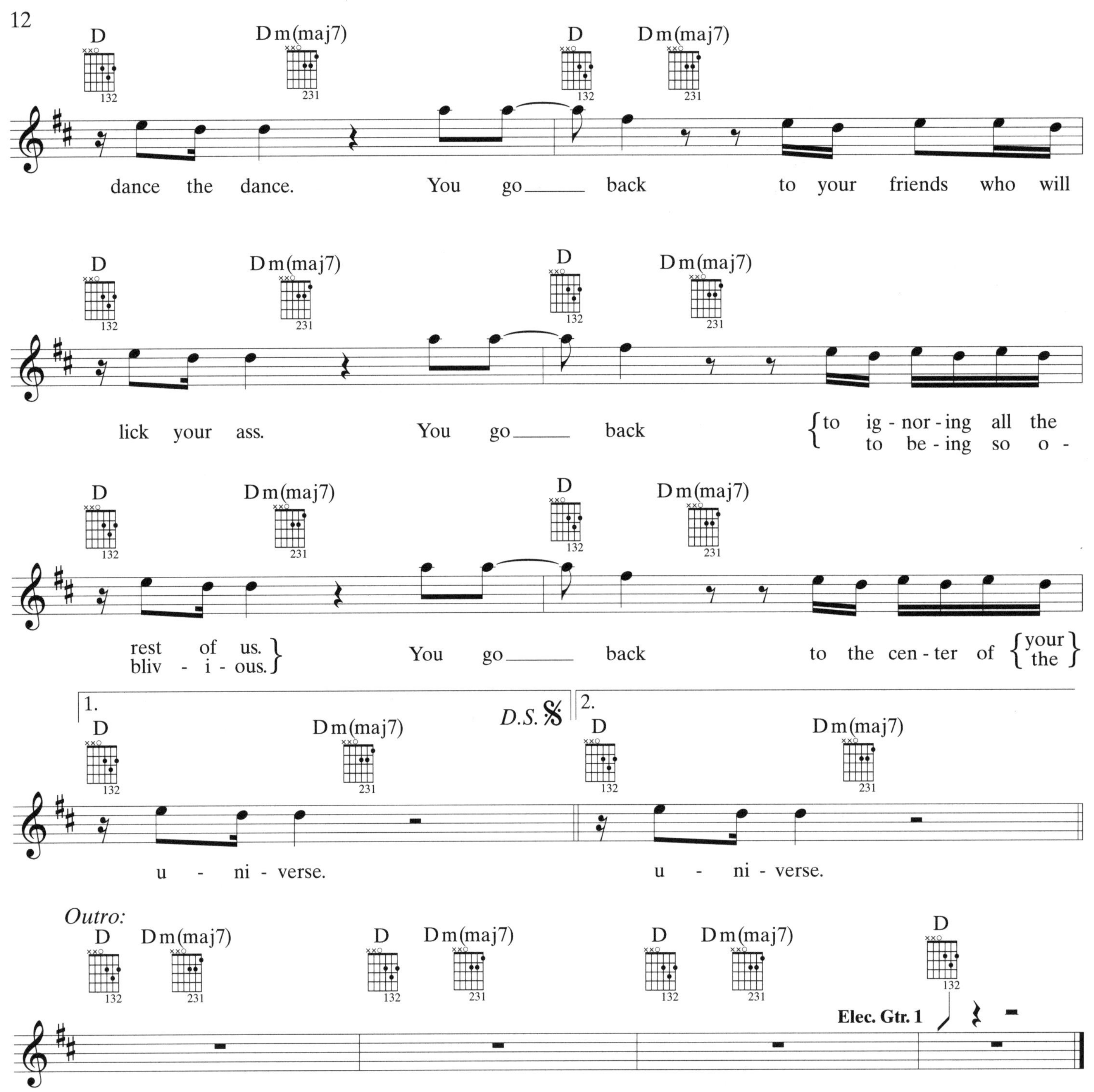

Verse 3:
Dear self-centered boy,
I don't know why I still feel affected by you.
I've never lasted very long with someone like you,
I never did although I have to admit I wanted to.
Dear magnetic boy,
You've never been with anyone who doesn't take your shit.
You've never been with anyone who dared to call you on it,
I wonder how you'd be if someone were to call you on it.

Pre-chorus 3:
And any talk of willingness,
And any talk of both feet in,
And any talk of commitment
Leaves you running for the door.
(To Chorus:)

HANDS CLEAN

Words and Music by
ALANIS MORISSETTE

© 2002 Universal - MCA Music Publishing, A Division of Universal Studios, Inc. and 1974 Music
All Rights Controlled and Administered by Universal - MCA Music Publishing,
A Division of Universal Studios, Inc.
All Rights Reserved

Pre-chorus:
C(9)
D5
G/B
C(9)
D5
Acous. Gtr. 1
cont. rhy. simile
Ooh, this could be mess - y, but you don't
Elec. Gtr. 1
Elec. Gtr. 1 cont. simile
T
A
B
12 13 12 13 14 15 14 15
10 12 10 12 12 13 12 13
G/B
C(9)
D5
G/B
C(9)
seem to mind. Ooh, don't go tell-ing ev - 'ry-bod - y
D5
G/B
C(9)
and o - ver - look this sup - pos - ed crime.
Chorus:
w/Rhy. Fig. 1 (*Elec. Gtr. 2) simile
D5
G/B
C(9)
Acous. Gtr. 1 cont. rhy. simile
We'll fast for - ward to a few years lat - er and
*w/distortion.
D5
G/B
C(9)
and no one knows ex - cept the both of us.

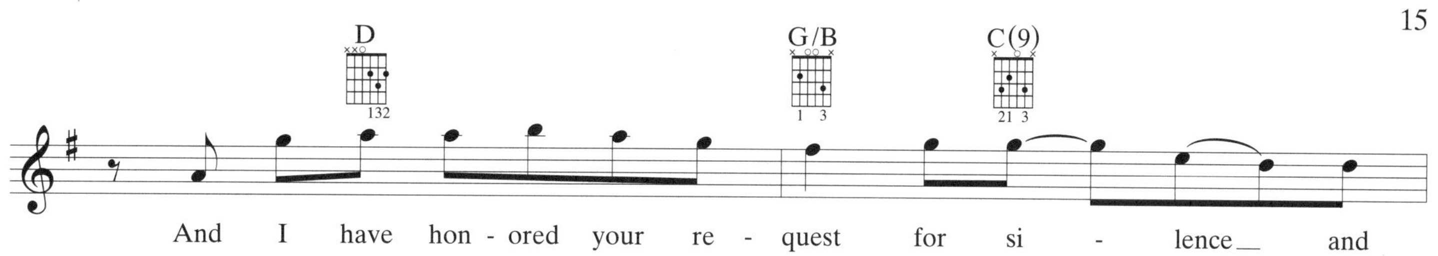
D
G/B
C(9)
And I have hon - ored your re - quest for si - lence and

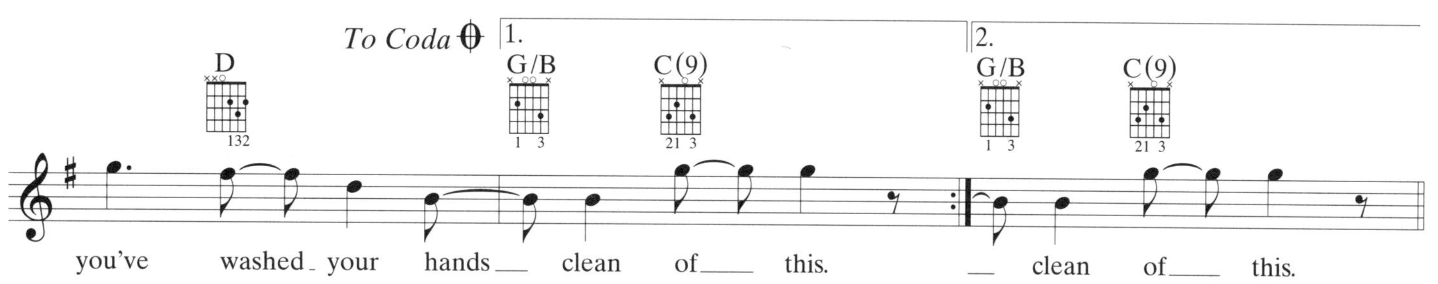
To Coda
1.
2.
D
G/B
C(9)
G/B
C(9)
you've washed your hands clean of this. clean of this.

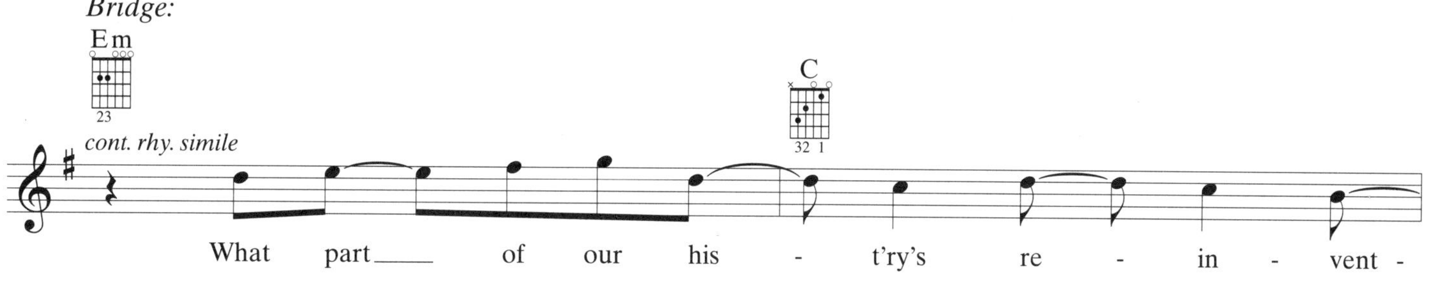
Bridge:
Em
C
cont. rhy. simile
What part of our his - t'ry's re - in - vent -

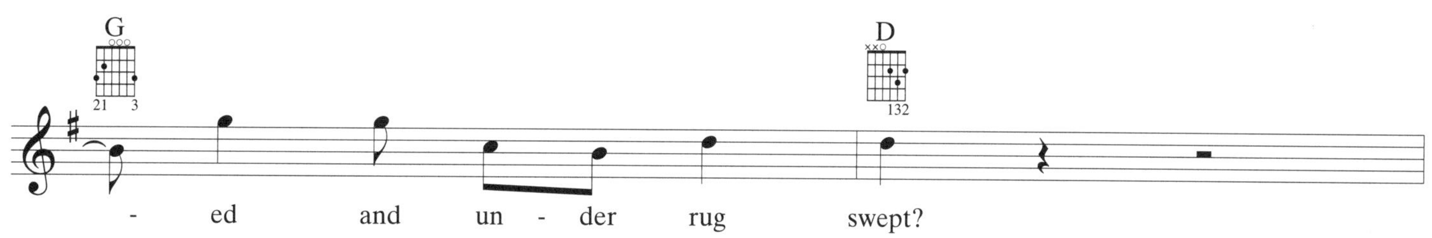
G
D
- ed and un - der rug swept?

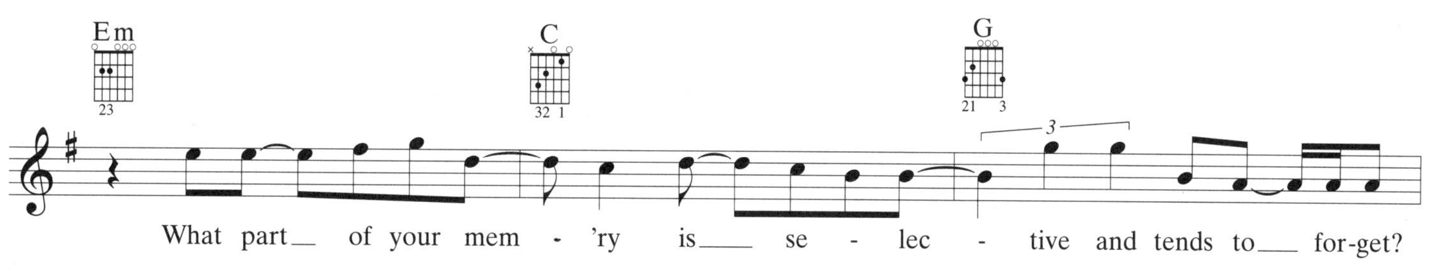
Em
C
G
What part of your mem - 'ry is se - lec - tive and tends to for-get?

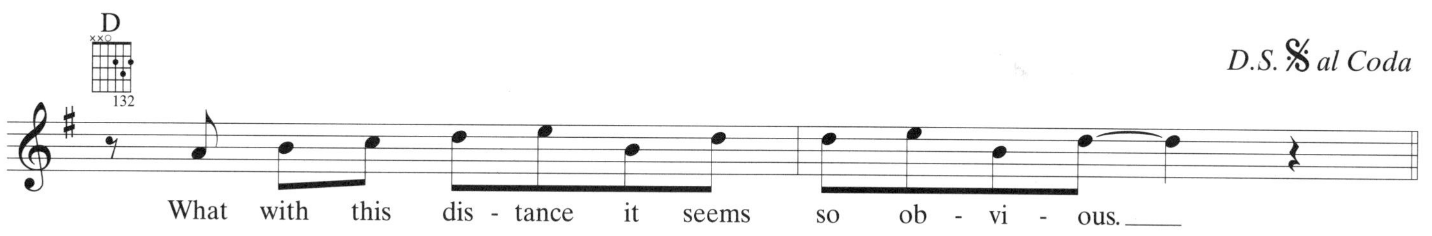
D
D.S. al Coda
What with this dis - tance it seems so ob - vi - ous.

Verse 3:
Just make sure you don't tell on me, especially to members of your family.
We best keep this to ourselves and not tell any members of our inner posse.
I wish I could tell the world cuz you're such a pretty thing when you're done up properly.
I might want to marry you one day if you watch that weight and keep your firm body.
(To Pre-chorus:)

FLINCH

Words and Music by
ALANIS MORISSETTE

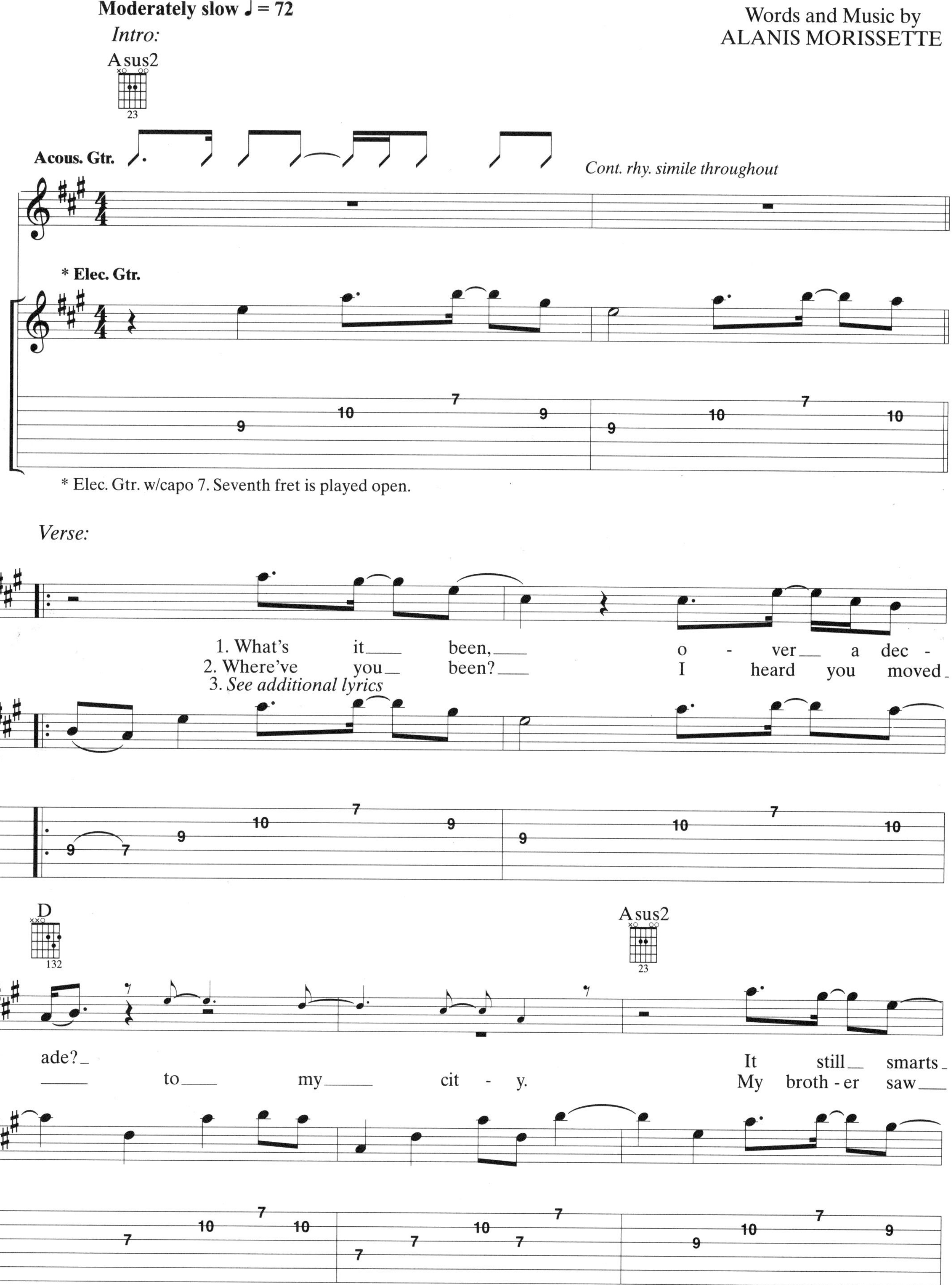

© 2002 Universal - MCA Music Publishing, A Division of Universal Studios, Inc. and 1974 Music
All Rights Controlled and Administered by Universal - MCA Music Publishing,
A Division of Universal Studios, Inc.
All Rights Reserved

D
E
F
4fr.
5fr.
132
Acous. Gtr.
like it was four min-utes a - go.
you some - where down - town.
9 9 10 9 7
7 10 7 10
7 7 10
Asus2
23
Resume verse fig. (both gtrs.) simile
We on - ly in - flu-enced each oth - er to - tal - ly.
I'd be par - a - lyzed if I ran in - to you.
We on - ly bruised each oth - er e - ven more
My tongue would sieze up if we were
Dm
231
so.
to meet a - gain.
1. What are you, my blood?
2. What are you, my god?
Pre-chorus:
You touch me like you are my blood.
You touch me like you are my god.
3. See additional lyrics

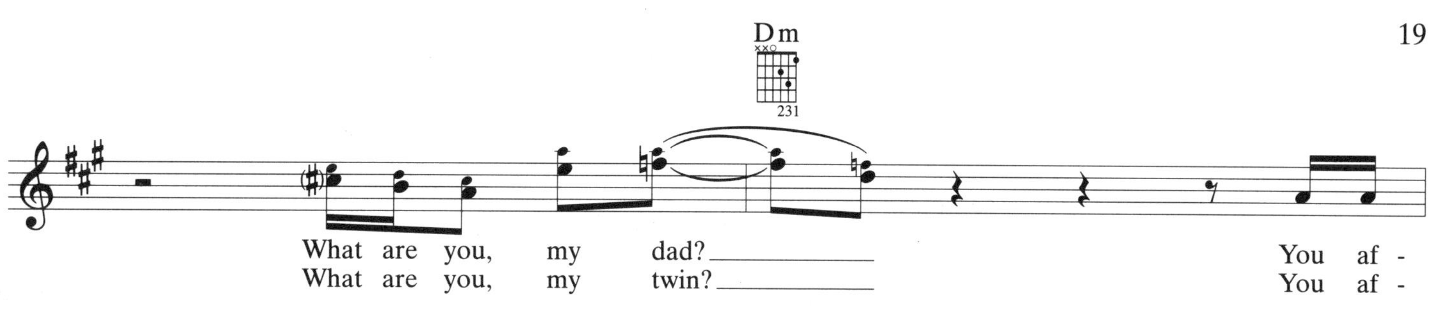
Dm
What are you, my dad?
What are you, my twin?
You af -
You af -

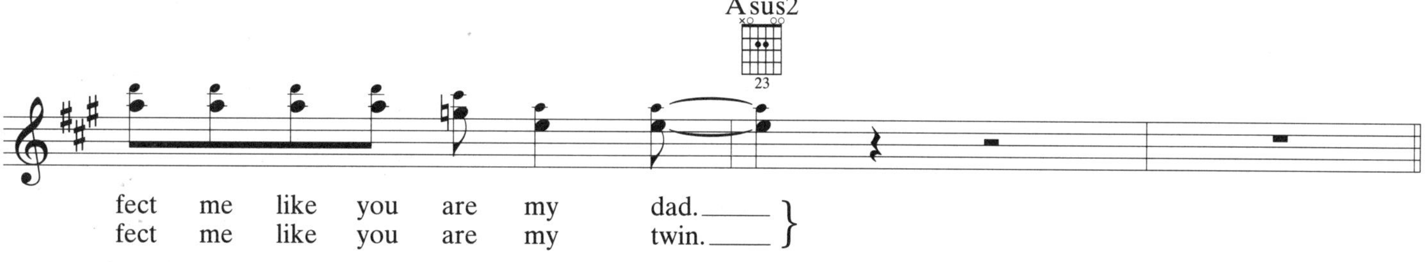
Asus2
fect me like you are my dad.
fect me like you are my twin.

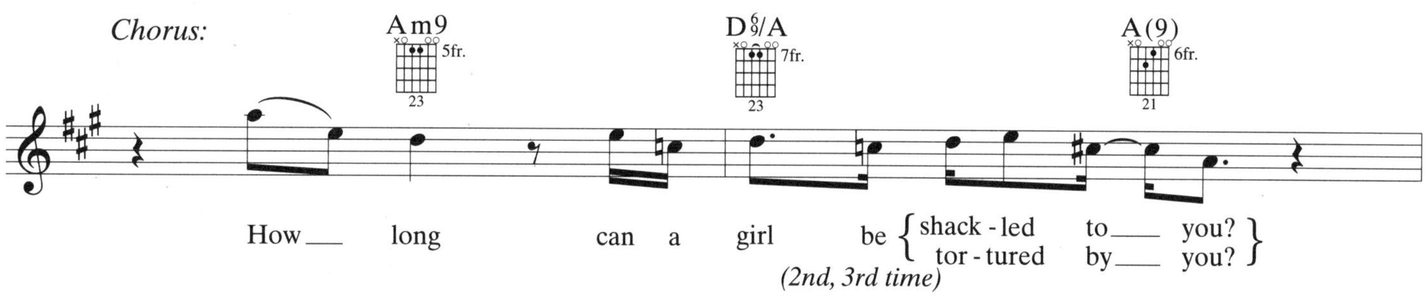
Chorus:
Am9
D6/9/A
A(9)
How long can a girl be shack-led to you?
tor-tured by you?
(2nd, 3rd time)

Asus2
Am9
D6/9/A
A(9)
How long be-fore my dig-ni-ty is re-claimed?

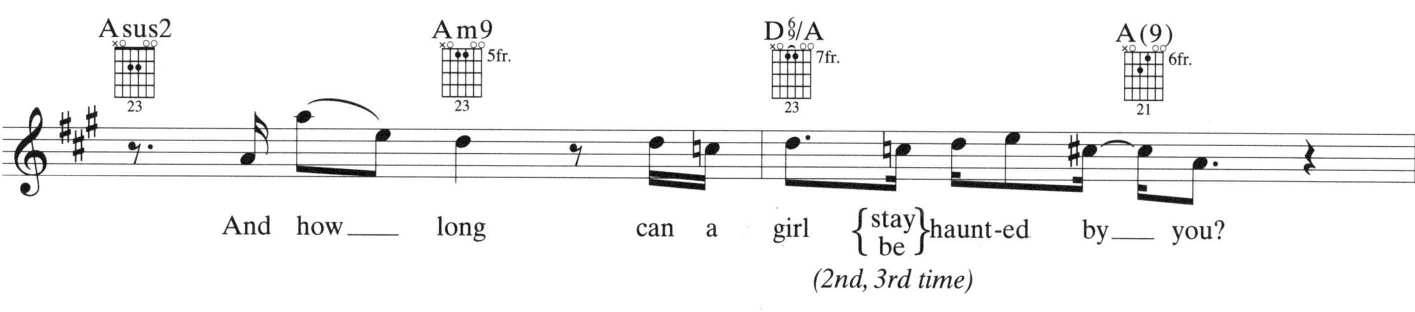
Asus2
Am9
D6/9/A
A(9)
And how long can a girl stay haunt-ed by you?
be
(2nd, 3rd time)

C
D
Asus2
Soon I'll grow up and I won't e-ven flinch at your name.

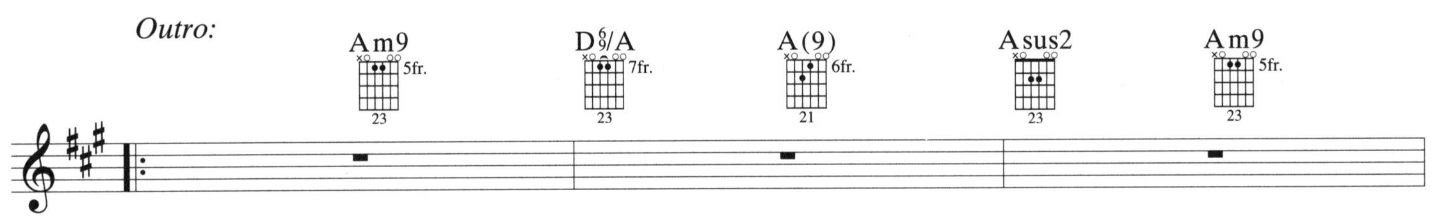

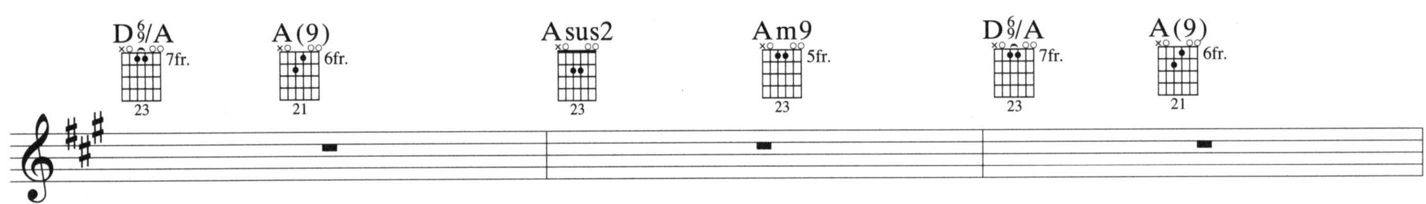

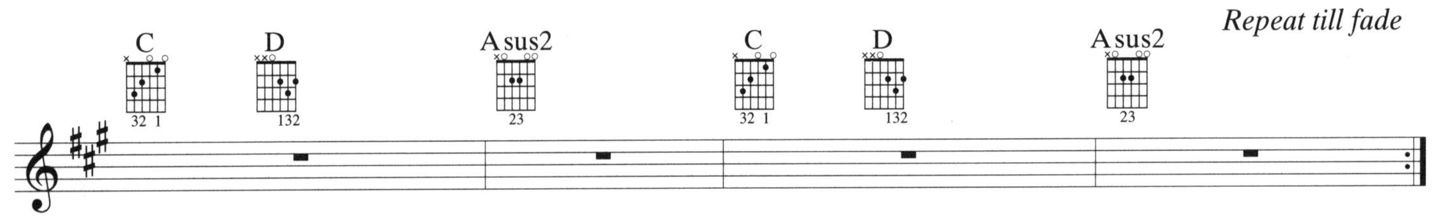

Verse 3:
So here I am one room away from where I know you're standing.
A well intentioned man told me you just walked in.
This man knows not of how this information has affected me.
But he knows the color of the car I just drove away in.

Pre-chorus 3:
What are you, my kin?
You touch me like you are my kin.
What are you, my air?
You affect me like you are my air.
(To Chorus:)

SO UNSEXY

Words and Music by
ALANIS MORISSETTE

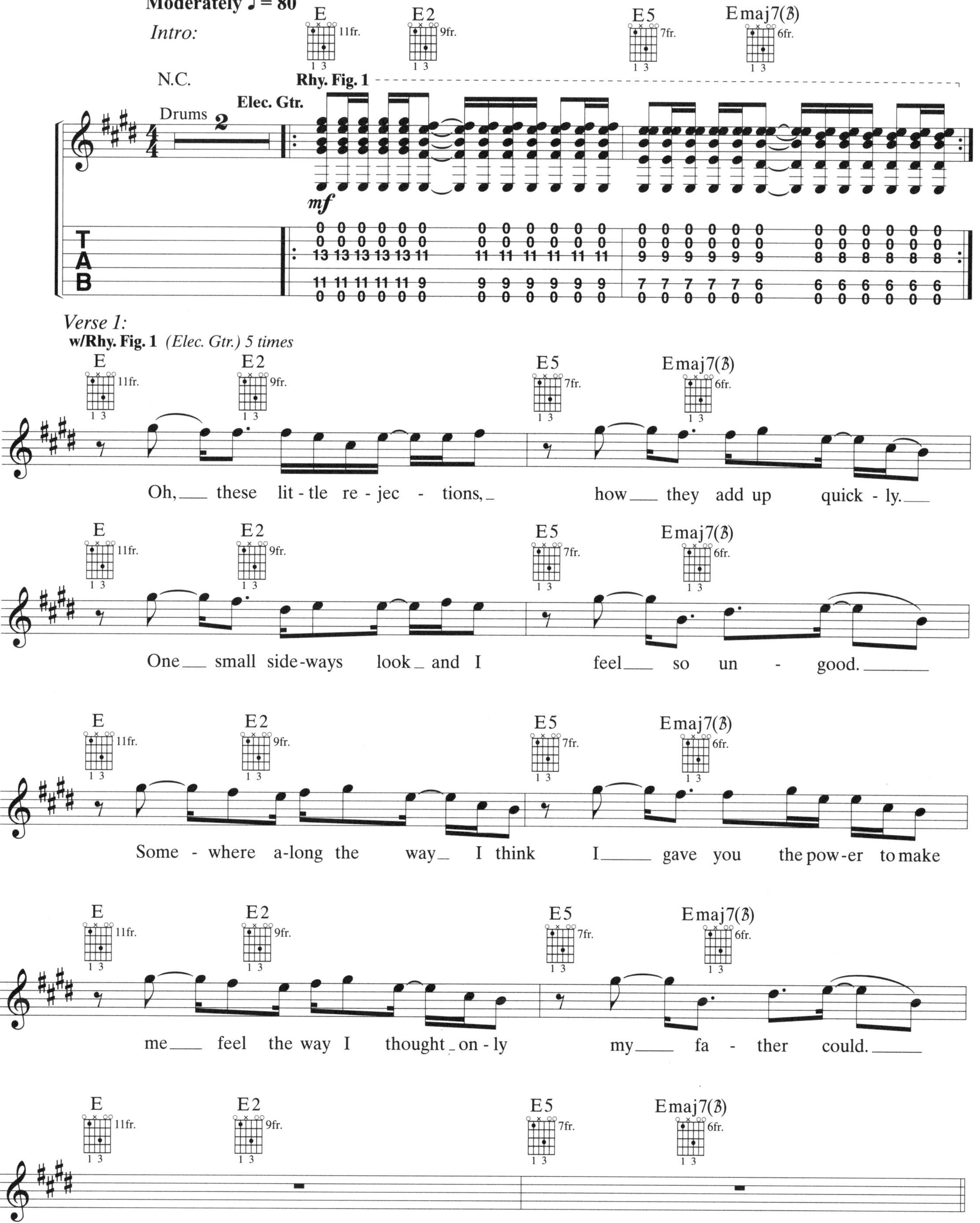

© 2002 Universal - MCA Music Publishing, A Division of Universal Studios, Inc. and 1974 Music
All Rights Controlled and Administered by Universal - MCA Music Publishing,
A Division of Universal Studios, Inc.
All Rights Reserved

Verses 2, 3, & 4:
w/Rhy. Fig. 1 (Elec. Gtr.) 5 times
E
E2
E5
Emaj7(♭3)
2. Oh these lit - tle re - jec - tions, how they seem so real to me.
3. Oh, these lit - tle pro - tec - tions, how they fail to serve me.
4. See additional lyrics
One for - got - ten birth - day I'm all! but cooked.
One for - got - ten phone call and I'm de - flat - ed.
How these lit - tle a - ban - don-ments seem to sting so eas - i - ly.
Oh, these lit - tle de-fens - es, how they fail to com - fort me.
I'm thir - teen a - gain, am I thir - teen for good?
Your hand pull - ing a - way and I'm dev - as - tat - ed.
I can feel
Chorus:
w/Rhy. Fig. 1 (Elec. Gtr.) 5 times
so un - sex - y for some - one so beau - ti - ful. So un - loved and for
some-one so fine. I can feel so bor - ing for some - one so in - ter - est-ing.

E
E2
To Coda
E5
Emaj7(♭3)
So ig - nor - ant for some - one of sound mind.
1.
2.
Bridge:
C
D
When will I stop leav - ing, ba - by?
When will I stop de - sert - ing, ba - by, yeah. When will I start stay - ing with my - self?
D.S. al Coda
Coda
some - one of sound mind. I can feel so un - sex - y for some - one so beau - ti - ful. So un - loved and for

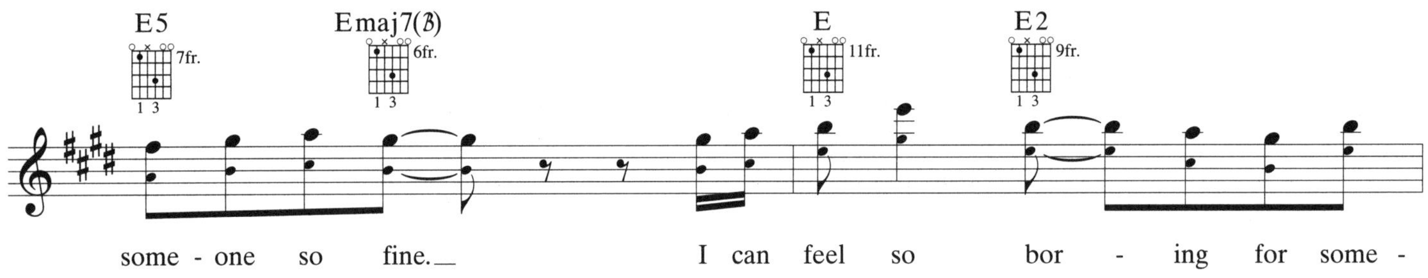

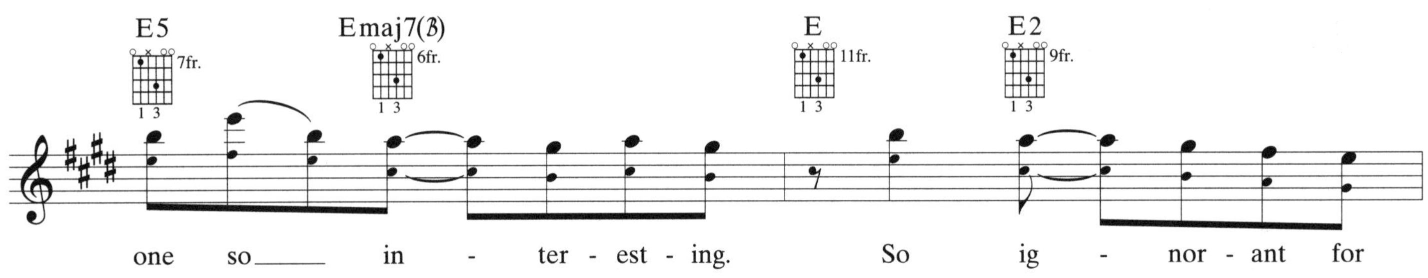

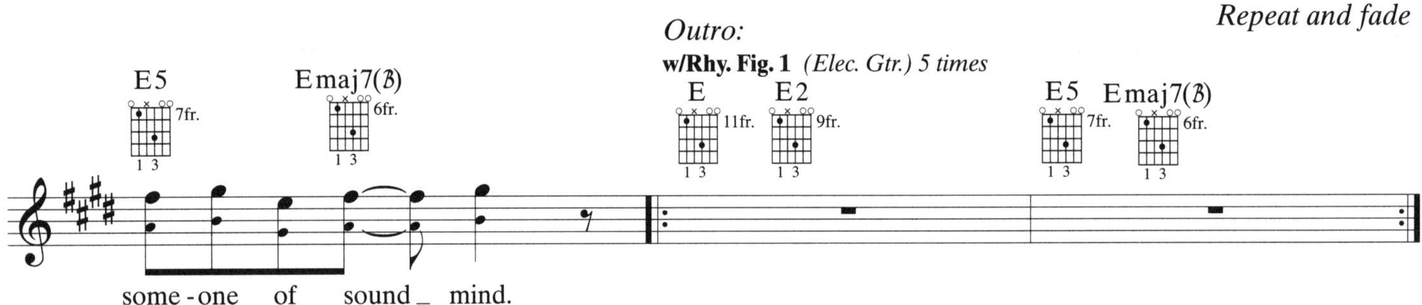

Verse 4:
Oh, these little projections,
How they keep springing from me.
I jump my ship as I take it personally.
And, oh, these little rejections,
How they disappear quickly
The moment I decide not to abandon me.
(To Chorus:)

Tune down 1/2 step:
⑥ = E♭ ③ = G♭
⑤ = A♭ ② = B♭
④ = D♭ ① = E♭

PRECIOUS ILLUSIONS

Words and Music by
ALANIS MORISSETTE

© 2002 Universal - MCA Music Publishing, A Division of Universal Studios, Inc. and 1974 Music
All Rights Controlled and Administered by Universal - MCA Music Publishing,
A Division of Universal Studios, Inc.
All Rights Reserved

D5 E5
- nal - ly___ be - gin.___ I'll be wor - thy, right?
___ knight in___ shin - ing___ ar - mour. This pill will help me yet
D5
On - ly when you re - al - ize___ the gem I am. But this
as will these boys___ gone__ through like wa - ter. But this
Pre-chorus:
E A D E A
won't work__ now__ the way___ it once did.__ And I won't keep it up___ e - ven though
won't work as well__ as the way___ it once did.__ Cuz I want to de - cide__ be-tween sur -
D E A
___ I would love__ to. Once I know who I'm not,___ then I'll know__
- viv - al and___ bliss. And though I know who I'm not,___ I still don't
D E A D E
__ who I am.__ But I know I won't keep__ on play - ing____ the vic - tim.
know who I am.__ But I know I won't keep__ on play - ing____ the vic - tim.
1.3. These pre-cious il - lu -
2. These pre-cious il - lu -
Chorus:
D A E
- sions in___ my head__ did not let me down___ when I____ was de - fense-
- sions in___ my head__ did not let me down___ when I____ was a kid.__
D A G D/F♯
- less. And part-ing with them___ is like part - ing with in - vis - i - ble___ best friends.__
___ And part-ing with them___ is like part - ing with a child - hood__ best friend.__

E
To Coda
1.
2.
3. This
Bridge:
A C G E A
I've spent so long firm - ly look - ing out - side me. I've spent so much
C G B
D.S. al Coda
time liv - ing in sur - viv - al mode. 3. But this
Coda
D A
These pre-cious il - lu - sions in my head did not let me down
E D A
when I was a kid. And part-ing with them is like part - ing with a
G D/F♯ E
child - hood best friend.
Outro:
D A E
Ooh, ooh.
D A G D/F♯ E

THAT PARTICULAR TIME

© 2002 Universal - MCA Music Publishing, A Division of Universal Studios, Inc. and 1974 Music
All Rights Controlled and Administered by Universal - MCA Music Publishing,
A Division of Universal Studios, Inc.
All Rights Reserved

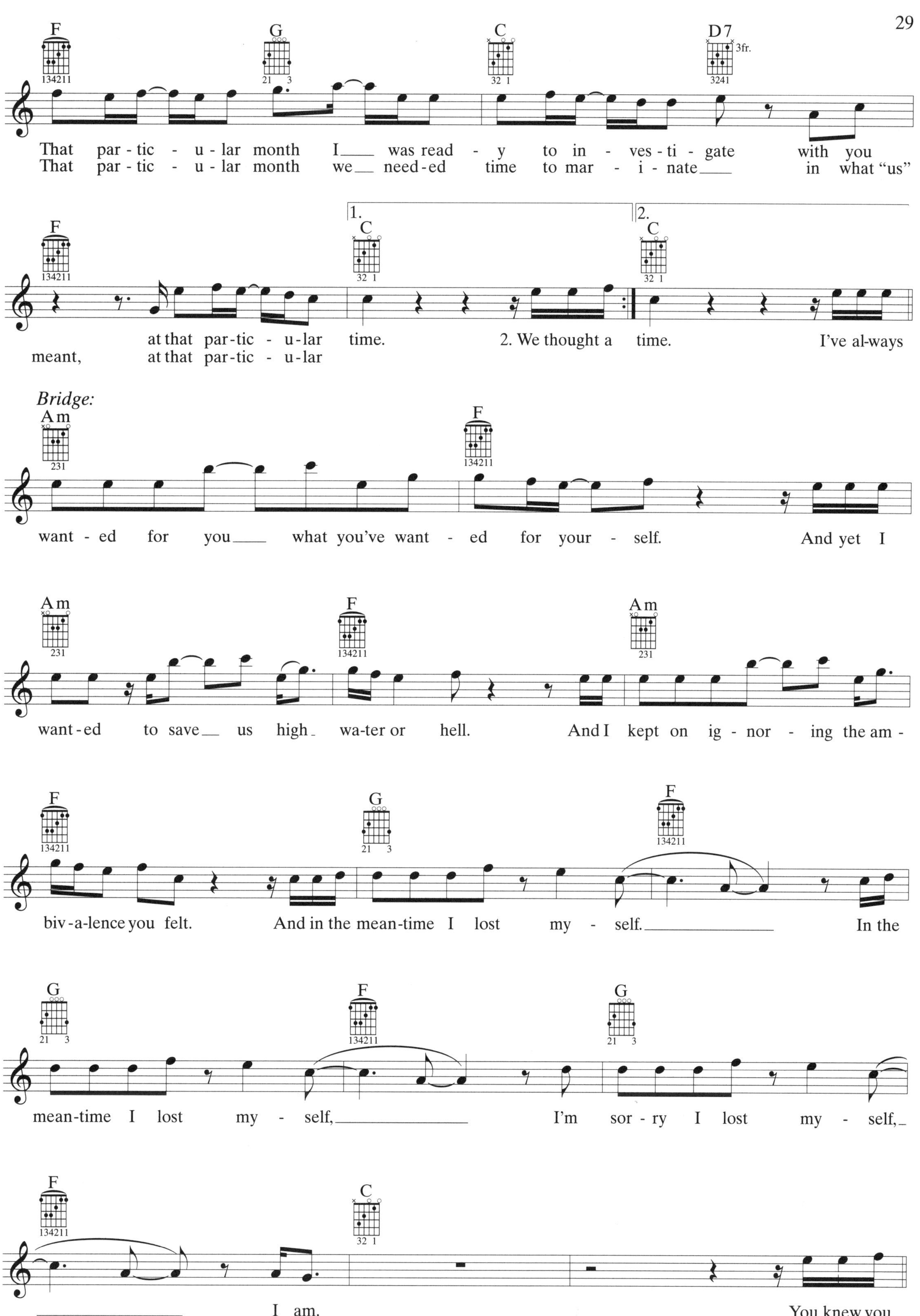
F G C D7
3fr.
That par-tic - u-lar month I was read - y to in - ves-ti - gate with you
That par-tic - u-lar month we need-ed time to mar - i - nate in what "us"
F
1. C
2. C
at that par-tic - u-lar time. 2. We thought a time. I've al-ways
meant, at that par-tic - u-lar
Bridge:
Am F
want - ed for you what you've want - ed for your - self. And yet I
Am F Am
want-ed to save us high wa-ter or hell. And I kept on ig - nor - ing the am -
F G F
biv-a-lence you felt. And in the mean-time I lost my - self. In the
G F G
mean-time I lost my - self, I'm sor-ry I lost my - self,
F C
I am. You knew you

Verse 3:
F
134211
Em
23
need - ed more time. time spent a - lone with no dis-trac-tion.
Dm
231
C
32 1
F
134211
You felt you need - ed to fly. so - lo and high
Dm
231
G
21 3
to de - fine what you want - ed. At
F
134211
G
21 3
C
32 1
D7
3fr.
3241
that par - tic - u - lar time love en - cour-aged me to leave. At
F
134211
G
21 3
C
32 1
that par - tic - u - lar mo - ment I knew stay-ing with you meant de-sert-ing me.
F
134211
G
21 3
C
32 1
D7
3fr.
3241
That par - tic - u - lar month was hard - er than you'd be - lieve but I still left
F
134211
C
32 1
at that par-tic - u-lar time.

A MAN

Words and Music by
ALANIS MORISSETTE

© 2002 Universal - MCA Music Publishing, A Division of Universal Studios, Inc. and 1974 Music
All Rights Controlled and Administered by Universal - MCA Music Publishing,
A Division of Universal Studios, Inc.
All Rights Reserved

years I have grov - eled, re - pen - tance ig -
of - ten re - mind - ed of the fools I'm a -
Pre-chorus:
w/Rhy. Fig. 1 (Elec. Gtr. 1) 8 times
w/Rhy. Fill 1 (Elec. Gtr. 2) 4 times, 2 & 3rd times only
Am/E*
Em
nored. 1.3. And I have been blamed, and
mong. 2. And I have been shamed, and
*Bass plays E.
Am/E*
Em
Am/E*
I have re - pent - ed. I'm work - ing my
I have re - lent - ed. I'm work - ing my
Em
D/E
1.
Em
way to - ward our un - ion mend - ed.
way to - ward our un - ion
2.3.
Em
Am/E*
Em
(2.) mend - ed. And I have been shamed, and
(3.) mend - ed. And we have been blamed, and

Am/E*
Em
I have re - pent - ed. I'm
we have re - pent - ed. I'm
Am/E*
Em
work - ing my way to - ward
work - ing my way to - ward
D/E
Em
our un - ion mend - ed.
our un - ion mend - ed.
Chorus:
C/E*
B7/E*
We don't fare well with end -
*Bass plays E.
Am/E*
Em
- less rep - ri - mands.
C/E*
B7/E*
We don't do well with a life
Am/E*
Em
served as a sen - tence.

Verse 3:
I am a man who still does what he can
To dispel our archaic reputation.
I am a man who has heard all he can,
Cuz I don't fare well with endless punishment.
Cuz…
(To Pre-chorus 3:)

YOU OWE ME NOTHING IN RETURN

© 2002 Universal - MCA Music Publishing, A Division of Universal Studios, Inc. and 1974 Music
All Rights Controlled and Administered by Universal - MCA Music Publishing,
A Division of Universal Studios, Inc.
All Rights Reserved

F
134211
times in your life and I won't judge it.
an-y-thing at all, and I'll un-der-stand it.
You owe me
(And there are no strings at-tached to it.)
Chorus:
Am
231
3
noth - ing for giv - ing the love that I give. You owe me
T
A
B
G
21 3
Am
231
noth - ing for car - ing the way that I have. I give you
G
21 3
To Coda
thanks for re-ceiv-ing, it's my priv - i-lege. And you owe me noth-ing in re -

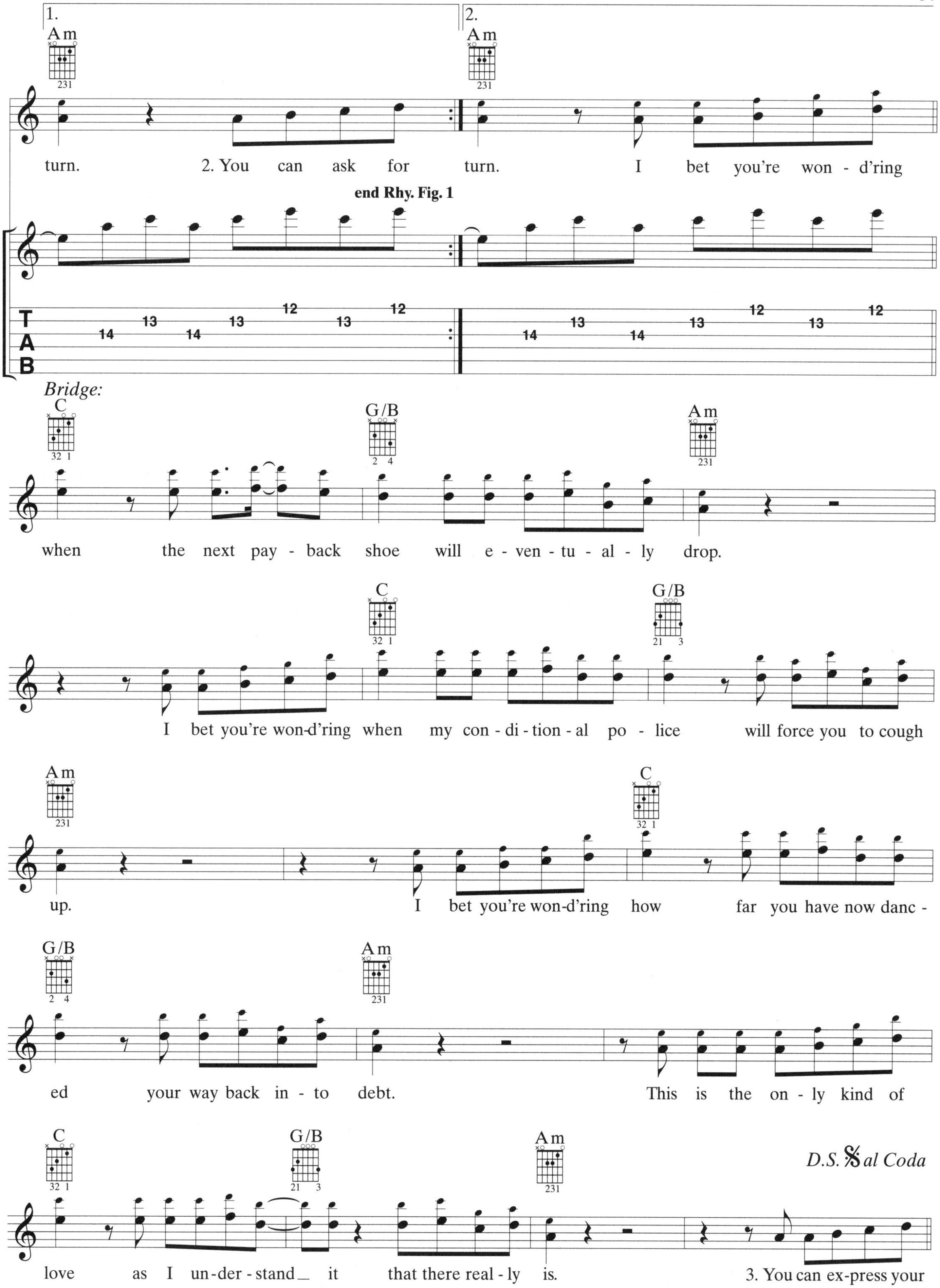

1. Am | 2. Am

turn. 2. You can ask for turn. I bet you're won - d'ring

end Rhy. Fig. 1

T A B
14 13 14 13 12 13 12 | 14 13 14 13 12 13 12

Bridge:

C G/B Am

when the next pay - back shoe will e - ven - tu - al - ly drop.

C G/B

I bet you're won-d'ring when my con - di - tion - al po - lice will force you to cough

Am C

up. I bet you're won-d'ring how far you have now danc -

G/B Am

ed your way back in - to debt. This is the on - ly kind of

C G/B Am

D.S. 𝄋 al Coda

love as I un-der - stand_ it that there real - ly is. 3. You can ex-press your

Coda

Am

w/Rhy. Fig. 1 *(Elec. Gtr.) simile*

turn. You owe me noth-ing_ for giv-ing the love that_ I give. You owe me

G Am

noth-ing_ for car-ing the way___ that I have. I give you thanks for_ re-ceiv-ing,_ it's

G Am

my priv-i-lege. And you owe_ me noth-ing in re-turn.

Outro:

G Am

G Am

Repeat and fade

Verse 3:
You can express your deepest of truths even if it means I'll lose you and I'll hear it.
You can fall into the abyss on your way to your bliss, I'll empathize with.
You can say that you have to skip town to chase your passion and I'll hear it.
You can even hit rock bottom, have a midlife crisis and I'll hold it.
(To Chorus:)

SURRENDERING

Words and Music by
ALANIS MORISSETTE

Moderately ♩ = 100

Intro:

N.C. (D)

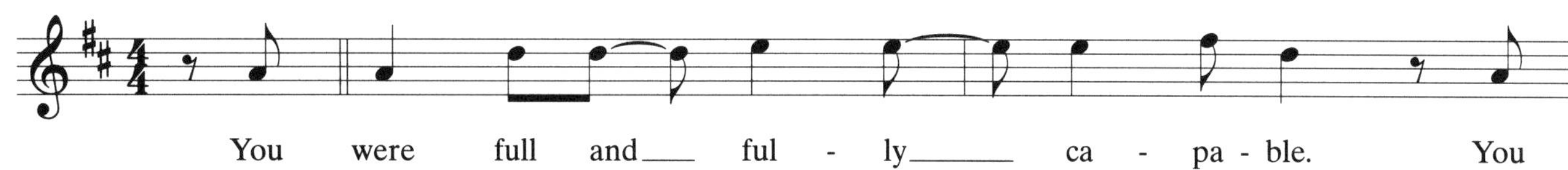

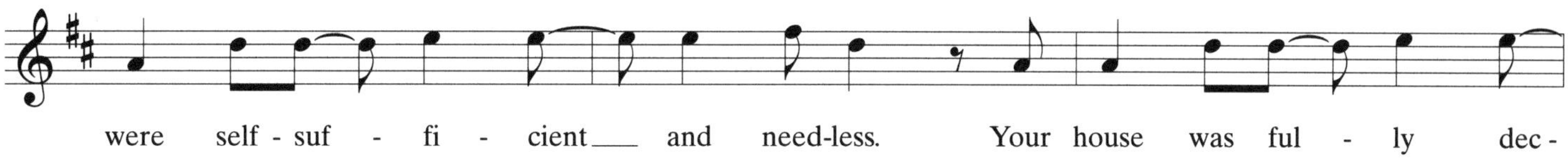

Verse:

w/Rhy. Fig. 1A *(Elec. Gtr. 1) 2nd & 3rd times only*

D

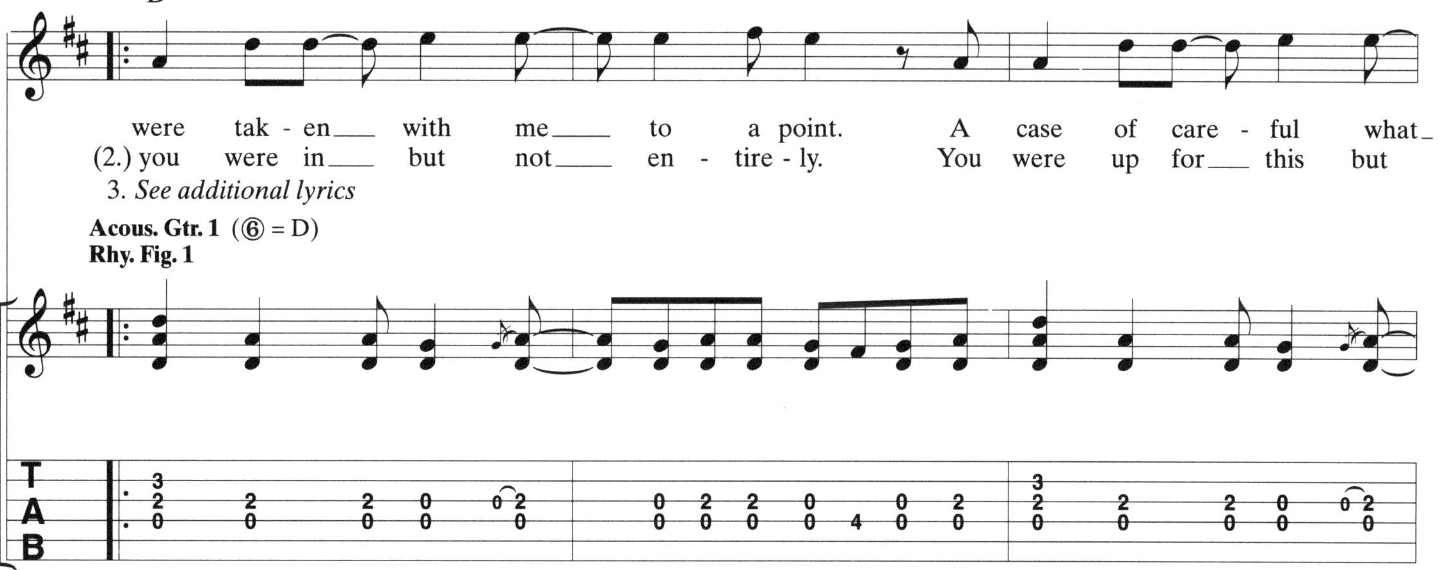

© 2002 Universal - MCA Music Publishing, A Division of Universal Studios, Inc. and 1974 Music
All Rights Controlled and Administered by Universal - MCA Music Publishing,
A Division of Universal Studios, Inc.
All Rights Reserved

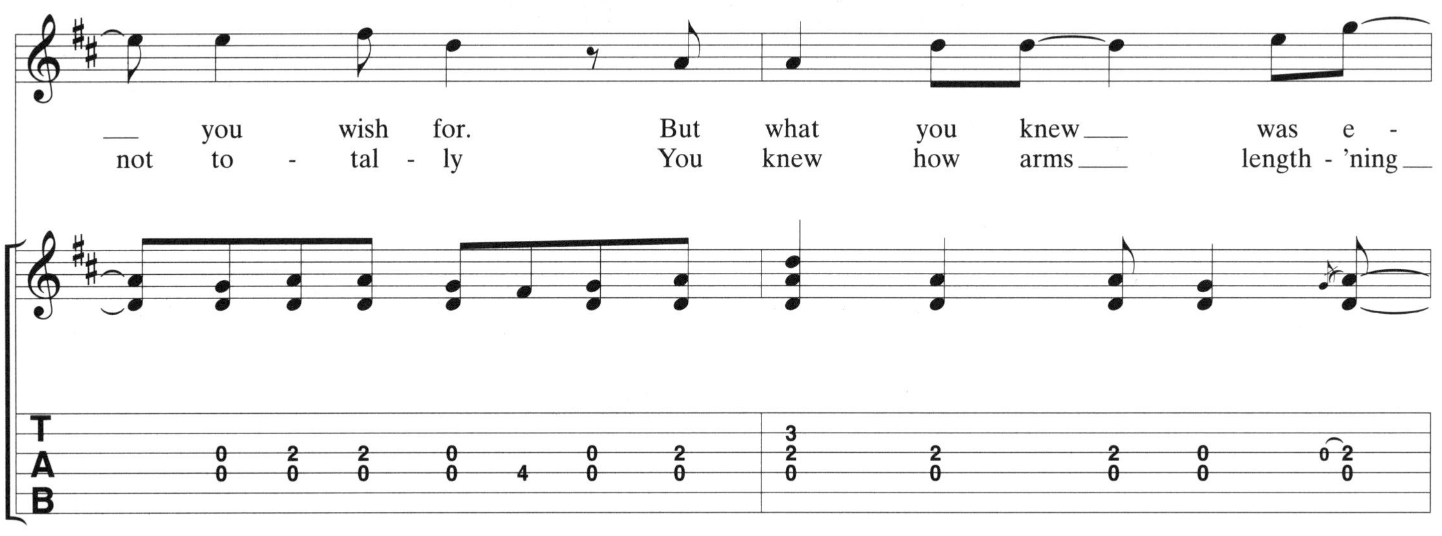
you wish for. But what you knew was e -
not to - tal - ly You knew how arms length - 'ning
T
A
B

- nough to be - gin. And so you called
can main - tain doubt. And so you fell
end Rhy. Fig. 1
T
A
B

Pre-chorus:
Acous. Gtr. 1 cont. Rhy. Fig. 1
and court - ed fierce - ly. So you reached out
and you're in - tact So you dove in
Elec. Gtr. 1 (Standard tuning)
Rhy. Fig. 1A
T
A
B

*Chorus:

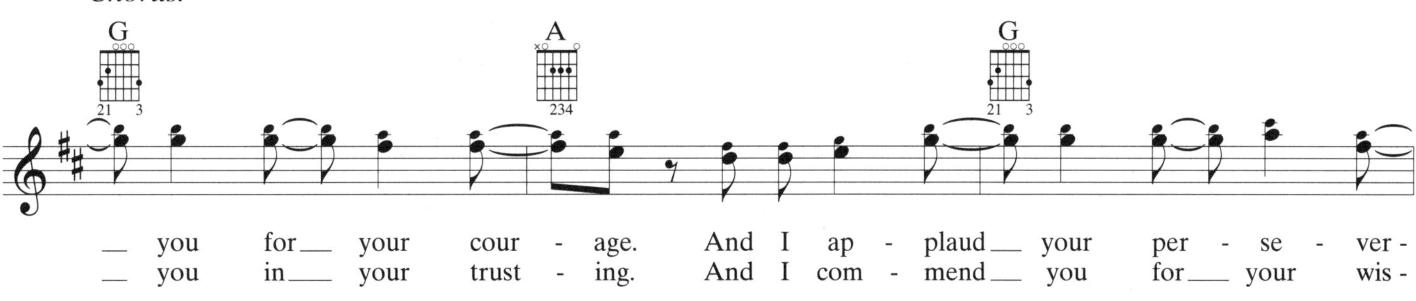

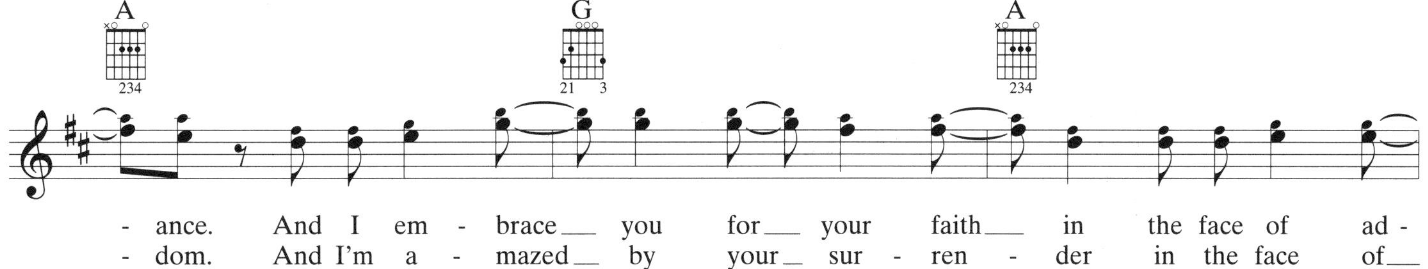

*Standard tuning frames for Elec. Gtr.

G
A
- ver - sar - i - al forc - es that I rep - re - sent.
threat - en - ing forc - es that I rep - re - sent.
w/Fill 1 (Elec. Gtr. 1)
w/Fill 2 (Elec. Gtr. 1) 2nd time only
1.2.
3.
Bridge:
D
Cmaj7
2. So
3. You
Self pro-tec-tion was in
G/B
Cmaj7
G/B
times of true dan-ger. Your best de-fense to mis - trust and be war - y.
Am
G
D
Sur-ren-der-ing a feat of un - e-qualed meas-ure. And I'm thrilled to let you in.
O - ver - joyed to be, let in in kind. And I sa - lute
Fill 1
Elec. Gtr. 1 (1st and 3rd times)
Fill 2
Elec. Gtr. 1 (w/echo set exactly 1 beat later)

Verse 3:
You found creative ways to distance.
You hid away from much through humor.
Your choice of armor was your intellect.

Pre-chorus 3:
And so you felt and you're still here.
And so you died and you're still standing.
And so you softened and still safely in command.
(To Chorus:)

UTOPIA

Words and Music by
ALANIS MORISSETTE

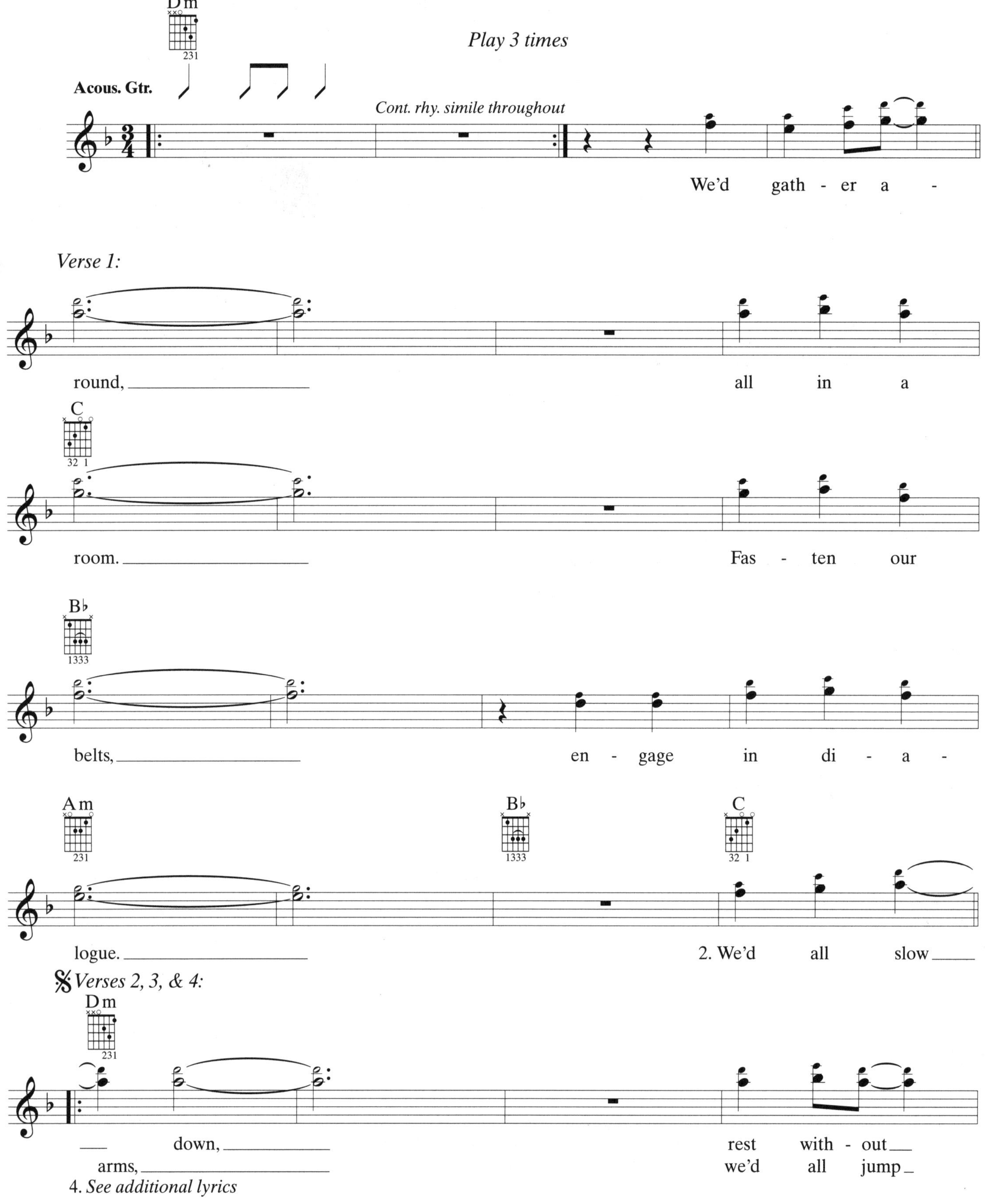

© 2002 Universal - MCA Music Publishing, A Division of Universal Studios, Inc. and 1974 Music
All Rights Controlled and Administered by Universal - MCA Music Publishing,
A Division of Universal Studios, Inc.
All Rights Reserved

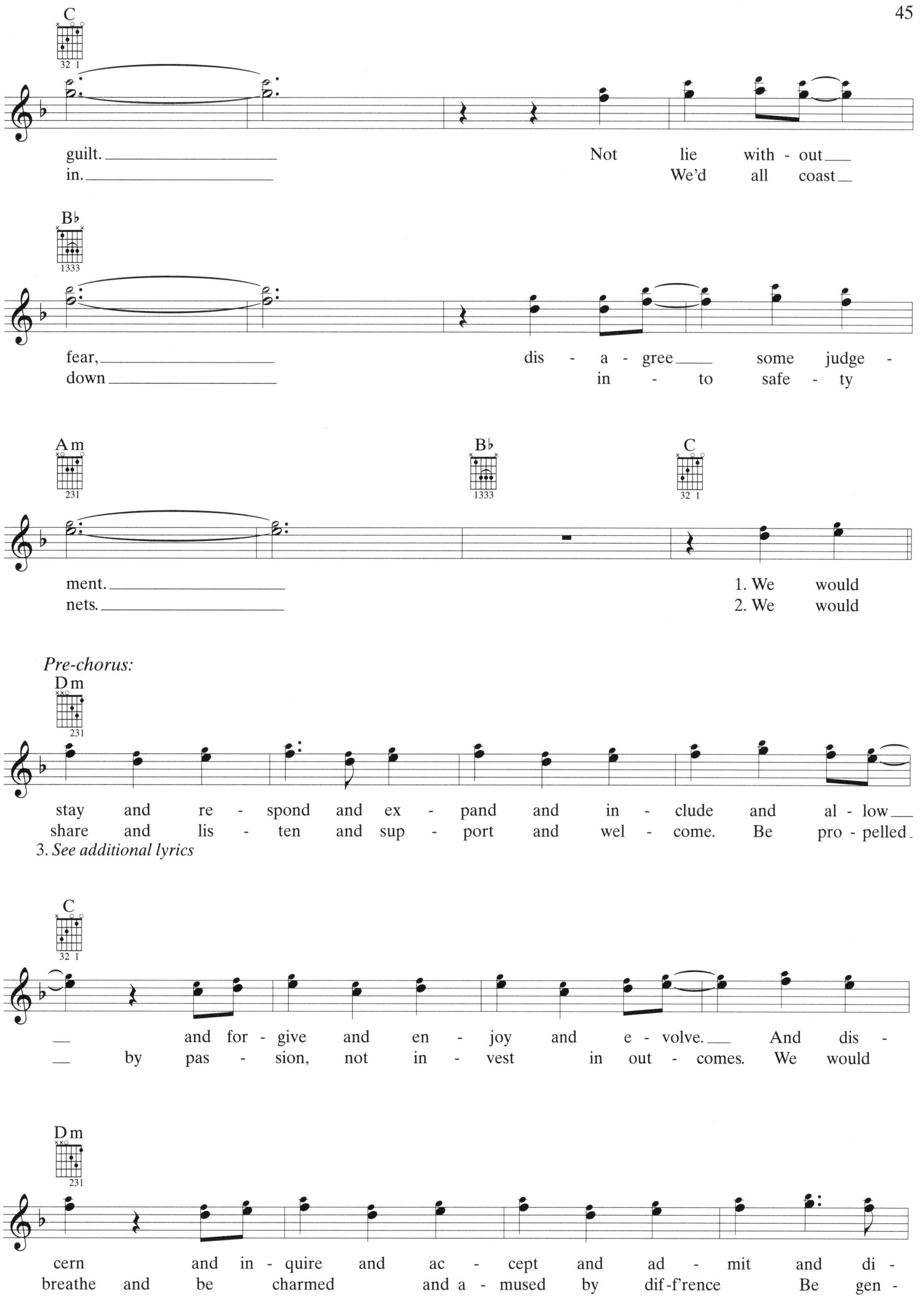
C
guilt. Not lie with - out
in. We'd all coast
B♭
fear, dis - a - gree some judge -
down in - to safe - ty
Am
ment.
nets.
B♭
C
1. We would
2. We would
Pre-chorus:
Dm
stay and re - spond and ex - pand and in - clude and al - low
share and lis - ten and sup - port and wel - come. Be pro - pelled
3. See additional lyrics
C
and for - give and en - joy and e - volve. And dis -
by pas - sion, not in - vest in out - comes. We would
Dm
cern and in - quire and ac - cept and ad - mit and di -
breathe and be charmed and a - mused by dif - f'rence Be gen -

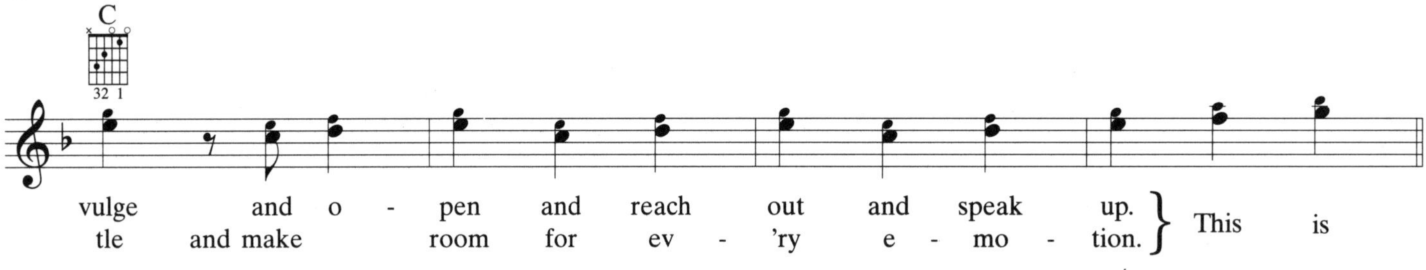
C
vulge and o - pen and reach out and speak up.
tle and make room for ev - 'ry e - mo - tion.
This is

Chorus:
F
u - to - pi - a, this is my

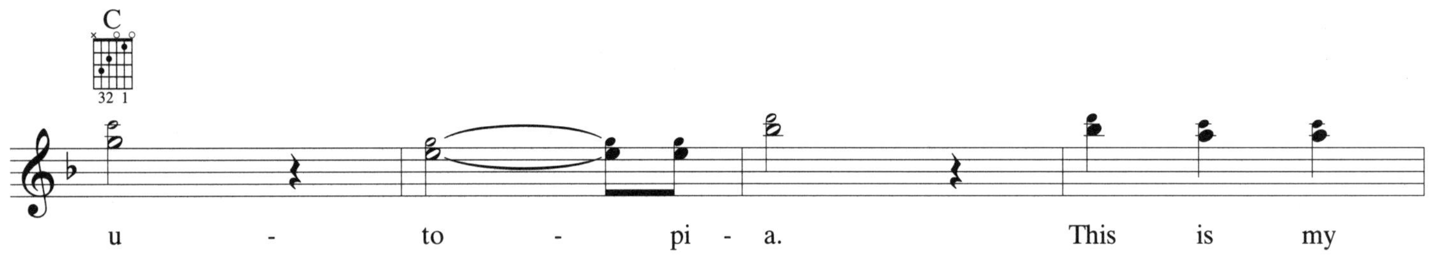
C
u - to - pi - a. This is my

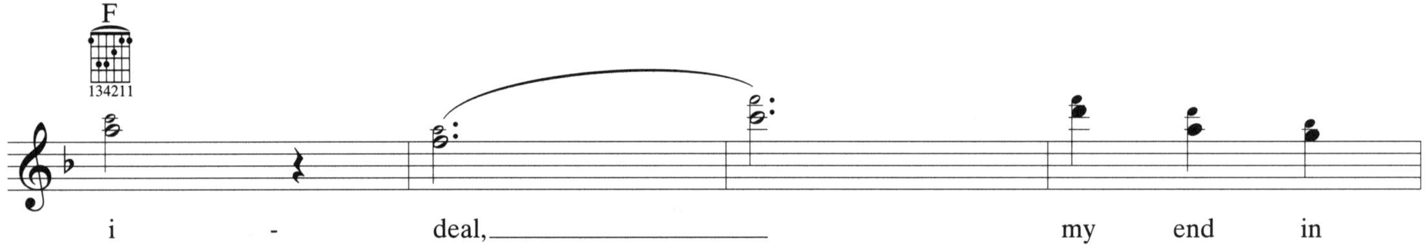
F
i - deal, my end in

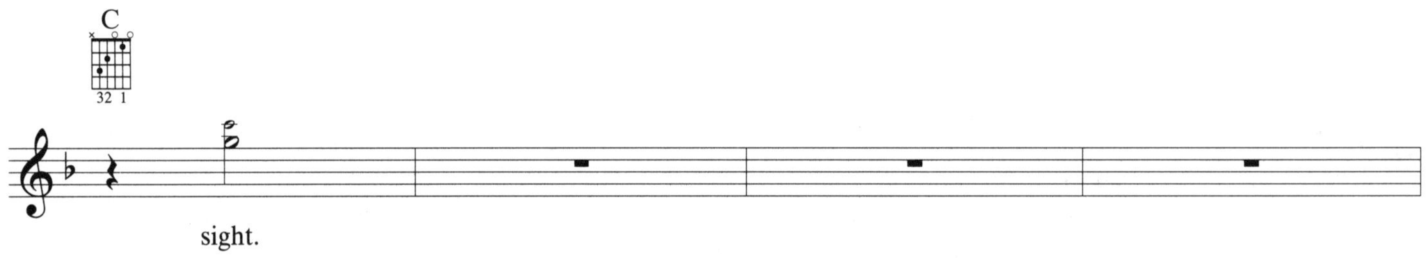
C
sight.

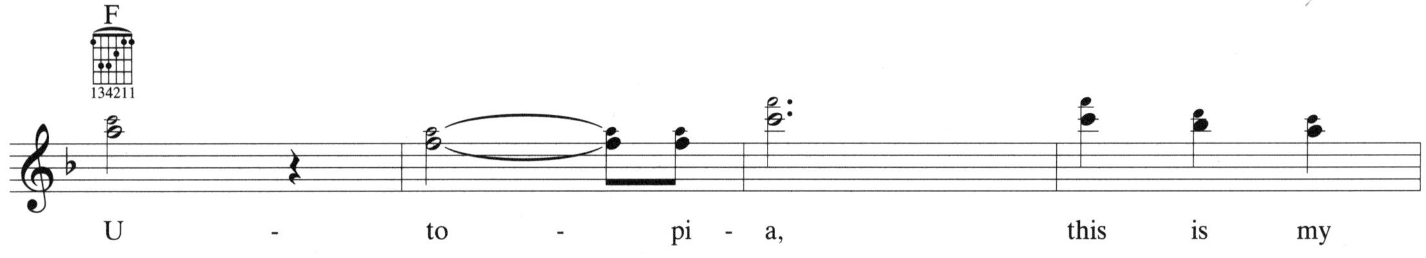
F
U - to - pi - a, this is my

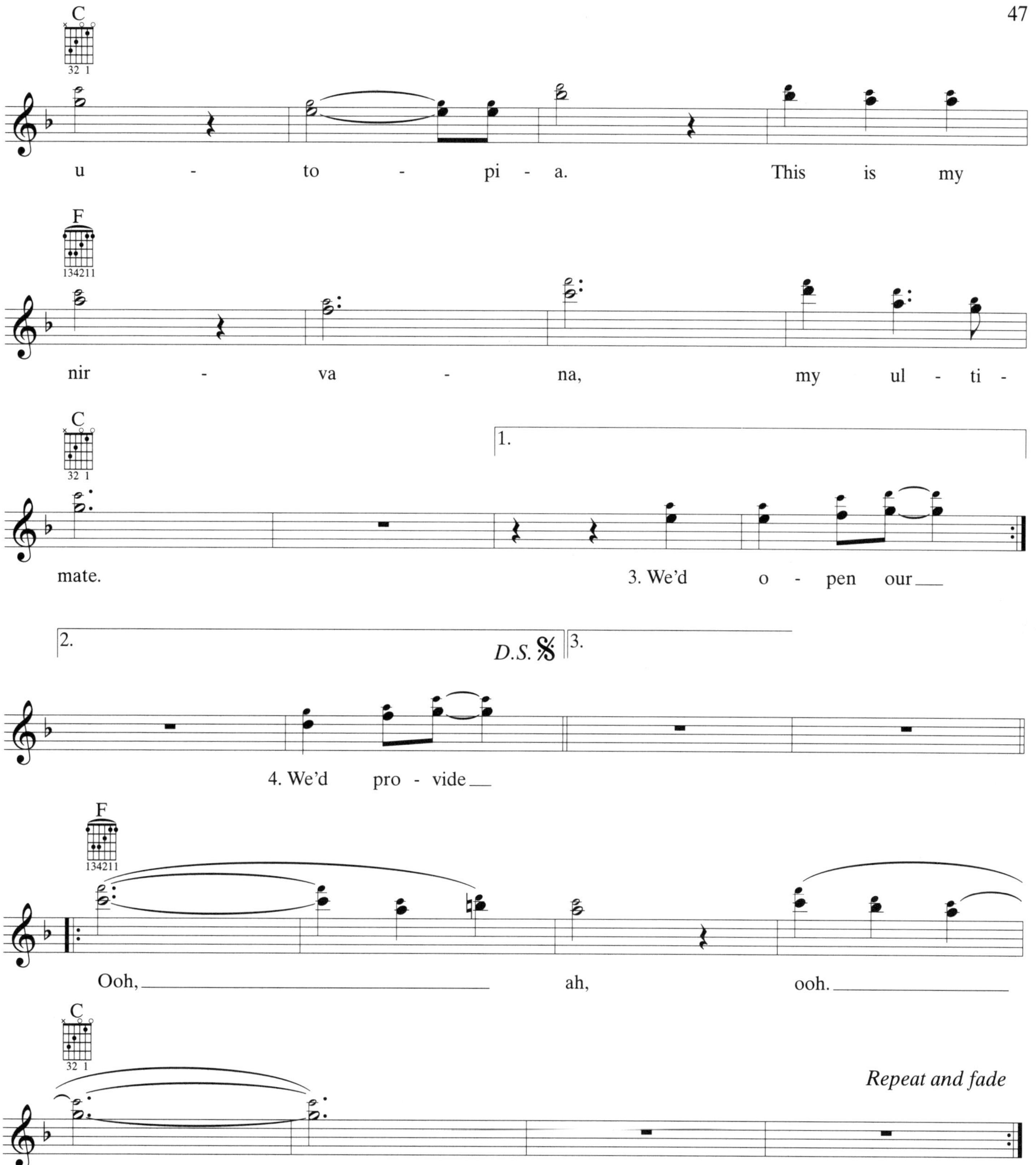

Verse 4:
We'd provide forums, we'd all speak out.
We'd all be heard, we'd all feel seen.

Pre-chorus 3:
We'd rise post-obstacle, more defined more grateful.
We would heal, be humbled, and be unstoppable.
We'd hold close and let go, and know when to do which.
We'd release and disarm and stand up and feel safe.
(To Chorus:)

GUITAR TAB GLOSSARY **

TABLATURE EXPLANATION

READING TABLATURE: Tablature illustrates the six strings of the guitar. Notes and chords are indicated by the placement of fret numbers on a given string(s).

BENDING NOTES

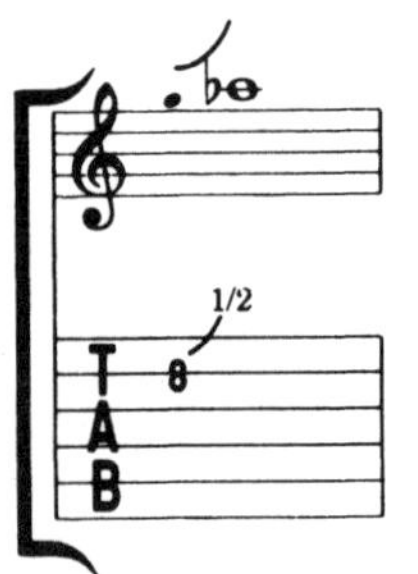

HALF STEP: Play the note and bend string one half step.*

WHOLE STEP: Play the note and bend string one whole step.

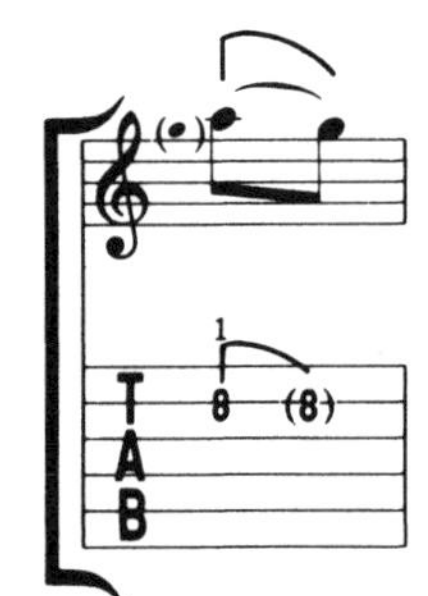

PREBEND AND RELEASE: Bend the string, play it, then release to the original note.

RHYTHM SLASHES

STRUM INDICATIONS: Strum with indicated rhythm.

The chord voicings are found on the first page of the transcription underneath the song title.

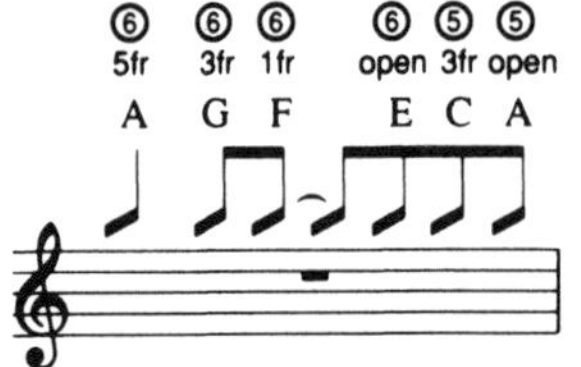

INDICATING SINGLE NOTES USING RHYTHM SLASHES: Very often single notes are incorporated into a rhythm part. The note name is indicated above the rhythm slash with a fret number and a string indication.

*A half step is the smallest interval in Western music; it is equal to one fret. A whole step equals two frets.

**By Kenn Chipkin and Aaron Stang

ARTICULATIONS

HAMMER ON: Play lower note, then "hammer on" to higher note with another finger. Only the first note is attacked.

PULL OFF: Play higher note, then "pull off" to lower note with another finger. Only the first note is attacked.

LEGATO SLIDE: Play note and slide to the following note. (Only first note is attacked).

PALM MUTE: The note or notes are muted by the palm of the pick hand by lightly touching the string(s) near the bridge.

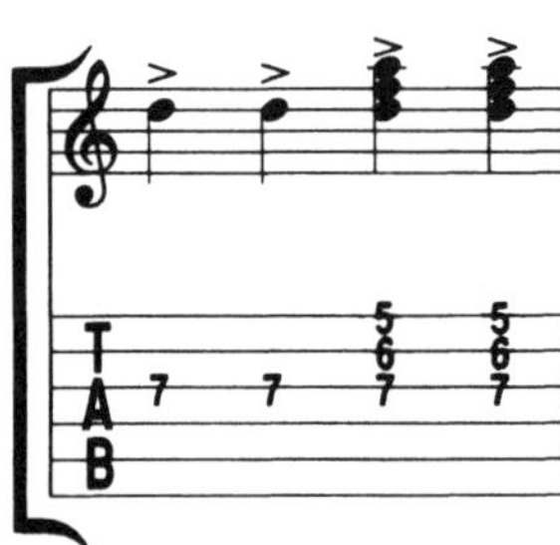

ACCENT: Notes or chords are to be played with added emphasis.

DOWN STROKES AND UPSTROKES: Notes or chords are to be played with either a downstroke (⊓.) or upstroke (v) of the pick.